HAUNTED
MONTICELLO,
FLORIDA

HAUNTED MONTICELLO, FLORIDA

Betty Davis and the Big Bend Ghost Trackers

Haunted
America

Published by Haunted America

A Division of The History Press

Charleston, SC 29403

www.historypress.net

All photos were taken by Kenneth A. Davis.

First published 2011

ISBN 978-1-5402-3039-3

Davis, Betty (Betty Gilbert)

Haunted Monticello, Florida / Betty Davis and the Big Bend Ghost Trackers.

p. cm.

ISBN 978-1-5402-3039-3

1. Ghosts--Florida--Monticello. 2. Haunted places--Florida--Monticello. I. Big Bend
Ghost Trackers (Team) II. Title.

BF1472.U6D37 2011

133.109759'87--dc22

2011015493

This book is dedicated to the citizens of Monticello, Florida—those who are living and those who have gone before.

CONTENTS

CONTENTS

ACKNOWLEDGEMENTS

As director-founder of Big Bend Ghost Trackers, I began my ghostly journey in Monticello in 2000. At a time before the many ghost-hunting reality television shows, it was not politically correct or always accepted to speak about the paranormal.

The citizens of Monticello welcomed me and my team with what the city is best known for: southern hospitality. From the mayor to the former sheriff, a congressman, attorneys, innkeepers, farmers, business and homeowners, rich or poor, educated or schooled from life's vast experiences, they all had credible and believable stories to tell of ghostly encounters.

Most importantly, I want to thank our spouses for all of their love and patience and for supporting us in our endeavor to write this book and realize a dream. This would not have been possible without them.

Michelle Cerdan, your team enthusiasm and group dedication makes you a valuable asset. Your research skills were invaluable to the writing of this book. You were there in the beginning and helped make Big Bend Ghost Trackers become what it is today. As the team's lead paranormal investigator, your keen knowledge is a major contributor to our many successful investigations.

Melanie Davis, your devotion to Historic Monticello Ghost Tours continues to make our tour north Florida's number one ghost tour. Your ability to capture "voices from the grave" is phenomenal, allowing our team to further validate the question: "Do our spirits live on after our earth bodies are no more?"

Christine McVicker, your team loyalty and tireless efforts, as well as your many hours of research and writing, have made this a reality. You are an up-and-coming professional psychic medium with incredible talent, and your connection to the afterlife provides a valuable tool for our team and a valuable service for those who want "one last time."

To the Monticello–Jefferson County Chamber of Commerce, Fran Hunt of the *Monticello News*, Pat Inmon and Jackie Andris, your support of Big Bend Ghost Trackers and Historic Monticello Ghost Tours is invaluable.

THE HISTORY OF JEFFERSON COUNTY

Jefferson County is situated in the heart of the Florida Panhandle, with its rolling hills and stately oaks draped in wispy Spanish moss. To the first-time visitor, the fictional town of "Mayberry" comes to mind. Youngsters walking down the red clay roads with fishing poles, lemonade stands set up in front yards, picnics in the park, church cakewalks and potluck suppers bring to mind a gentler time of a bygone era.

Shopkeepers and evening strollers kindly and willingly give strangers directions, recommend an eatery or assist with a flat tire. It's a place where neighbors have been known to borrow a cup of sugar from one another, bring a hot meal during times of sickness and sorrow and rejoice with each new birth. This is southern hospitality at its best. This is Monticello, Jefferson County, Florida.

Jefferson County is the only county in the state of Florida that extends all the way from Georgia on the north to the Gulf of Mexico on the south. Known as the "Keystone County," it is located about midway between Jacksonville, Florida's northernmost Atlantic port, and Pensacola, one of its largest Gulf ports.

Monticello, the county seat, is located just twenty-three miles east of Florida's capital, Tallahassee, and situated on U.S. Highways 19 and 90 directly off Interstate Highway 10.

With a population of just under fourteen thousand, Jefferson County is the home of a diverse population, vibrant culture and varying socioeconomic classes. Most of the downtown commercial buildings, in the Monticello Historic District, date from the last quarter of the nineteenth century. Listed on the National Register of Historic Places, Monticello also contains more than forty buildings dating from that century. These structures reflect the typical development of a north Florida town of the period. Unlike other Florida towns of the same era, nineteenth-century Monticello remains largely intact.

Jefferson County was founded in January 1827 and became the thirteenth county in territorial Florida. The county was named in honor of Thomas Jefferson, the third president of the United States of America, who served from 1801 to 1809. This happened eighteen years before Florida was admitted into the Union, on March 3, 1845, under the presidential administration of John Tyler. Florida entered into the statehood as the twenty-seventh state.

Six months before the founding of Jefferson County, on July 4, 1826, Thomas Jefferson died at his famous Virginia home, Monticello (pronounced *mont-i-chello*). The exact source of the name Monticello still remains a mystery today, though. Perhaps it was just providence when, a century later, descendants of Thomas Jefferson would be residents of the town for many years.

Monticello is located northeast of the county's center, at one of the highest points in western Florida, sitting at 236 feet above sea level. After Jefferson County was founded, five commissioners were called on to select the location for a permanent seat of justice. On August 15, 1827, the county seat was selected and named Monticello, likely in honor of Thomas Jefferson's famous home. Governmental offices were established, land was surveyed and lots for homes and businesses were sold. During the 1830s and 1840s, Monticello developed into the social, governmental and economic center of Jefferson County.

Jefferson County and Monticello have, over the years, had their share of trials and tribulations—such as the years of the Seminole Indian Wars, beginning in 1836, which brought death and destruction through attacks by hostile marauders on defenseless homes. The Civil War had brave boys in gray defending the state against the incursions of the enemy and fighting in all of the great battles of the war east of the Mississippi, under General Robert E. Lee. Following the war, the turbulent days of Reconstruction, the arrival of the carpetbaggers and post–Civil War fires destroyed much of the downtown area. The late spring cold wave of 1881 killed most of the farmers' crops. The yellow fever epidemic of 1888 left no family unaffected. But Jefferson County and Monticello prevailed.

By the time the turn of the century approached, Jefferson County residents had developed the saying "root hog or die," meaning that "we all must work hard to survive," and survive they did. Better days were coming in the form of watermelons. A local farmer by the name of William Cirardeau was instrumental in the cultivation of watermelons.

Before the mass production of watermelons began, early citizens gathered them from the edges of creek beds, where they grew wild. This method of gathering watermelons put local people unknowingly into contact with disease-carrying mosquitoes, which frequently left many of them ill with "fever 'n' ague," what we now know as malaria. Attributing their sickness to the watermelons, and not the insect, Jefferson County doctor John D. Palmer, who also owned an apothecary, educated the townspeople on the causes of malaria, having invented an elixir for its cure.

The first mass shipment of watermelon seeds was shipped to the Northeast in 1892, and for the next forty years, Jefferson County was able to expand this market, eventually producing 80 percent of the world's supply. In June 1949, the county began the tradition of hosting an annual Watermelon Festival.

As the years passed, one constant through all of the tragedies, turmoil and triumphs were tales of ghostly happenings; mysterious lights in cemeteries; doors opening and closing by unseen hands; ghostly faces appearing out of windows from long-abandoned houses; the sounds of ghostly footsteps; one street on which—be it the cold of January or the heat of August—the temperature is always cooler than on any other street; music emitting from empty buildings; and the residual sounds of a long-ago party. These tales have been handed down for generations from great-grandparents to grandparents to parents and, finally, to their children, and all are a part of local legends and folklore. Upon investigating these tales, one will discover that they are all an important part of local history.

Credible witnesses—a former sheriff, mayor, teachers, lawyers, middle-class housewives, shopkeepers and farmers—all have the same stories to share. Jefferson County and Monticello has an abundance of haunted locations.

The ghosts of early settlers, residents and movers and shakers of Jefferson County roam the town freely, perhaps from time to time unwittingly and unknowingly influencing the town's decision-makers of today.

In 2003, ABC News, based on the research, investigations and documentation of professional paranormal investigators the Big Bend Ghost Trackers, designated Monticello as the "South's Most Haunted Small Town." A plaque is proudly displayed in the Monticello–Jefferson County Chamber of Commerce with this distinction. One out of every three homes or businesses are presently haunted or have in the past experienced a haunting. The chamber of commerce is open from 9:00 a.m. to 4:00 p.m., Monday through Friday. All visitors are welcome.

OLD ST. MARGARITA'S CATHOLIC CHURCH

A church would be the one place that one would think would be *free* from experiencing a ghostly encounter, but that is not always the case. In Monticello, even an old church can play host to a ghost. It seems that although some members have left the earthly realm of life, they have perhaps never really left the church. Is it possible for members of a congregation to return happily to their old church?

The first Catholic church service was held in Monticello and Jefferson County in 1907, with a total of three professed Catholics in attendance, including Mrs. Charles Henry, Mr. Leo Majewski (a middle-aged gentleman) and his wife, Michalina. The Majewskis, having only recently arrived in the United States from Bremen, Germany, were Russian immigrants of Polish decent, with Leo being of noble blood.

With so few of Monticello's residents professing to be of the Catholic faith, to have a house of worship of their own seemed like an impossibility. Services were conducted at first in a room in the county courthouse, and then, as the congregation grew, the members would take turns hosting the services in their own homes and hotel parlors. By 1915, members of the sect had grown in numbers with the arrival of more Polish immigrants and other newcomers to the town. The dream of having a chapel of their own was becoming a reality.

People strolling by old St. Margarita's often hear phantom organ music coming from the old church. Here it looks the same as it did in 1915.

Funds were raised and provided by the individual members, led by Leo Majewski—being a devout Catholic, he was very instrumental and was the driving force in having Monticello's first Catholic church erected. Blessed and given the name St. Margarita's, the house of worship named Reverend Father Bresanham as the presiding priest.

The church was small and quaint, with impressive stained-glass windows. Leo spent most of his waking hours at the church. Having clerical skills, he served the church in many capacities. Michalina served the church with her talent as an organist. The church's choir loft was elevated, giving the choir members a clear view of everything happening at Mass, and the sound carried much better from the loft than from the other areas of the church building.

When helping to develop the plans and blueprints for the layout of the church, Leo had considered the placement of the choir. His thinking was that when a choir is located in front of the congregation, it appears that the choir is giving a concert instead of fulfilling its proper role at Mass—this was in keeping with the wishes of Pope Saint Pius X, who

The beautiful old church building from a bygone era plays host to two ghosts.

ordered in 1903 that choirs should be hidden behind screens or above the congregation. The pope's reasoning still stands today.

Over the years, a multitude of people worshiped at St. Margarita's and called it their spiritual home, none more faithful or devoted than Leo and Michalina. Many happy and prosperous years passed for Leo and Michalina. Although childless, their lives were in a state of wedded bliss in life, and in death they continued to be kindred spirits. Leo always promised his beloved that he would never leave her. Even before death, he assured her that he would still be near. When their golden years were upon them, Leo often recited a favorite work by the nineteenth-century poet Edna St. Vincent Millay to Michalina as a gesture of endearment—a poem simply called "Recuerdo," which, fittingly, means "remembrance": "We were very tired, we were very merry, we had gone back and forth all night on the ferry." Perhaps the poem sparked a memory of their arrival in their new land many years before; on their first night in their new country, they rode the ferryboat back and forth in the harbor.

When the spring of 1934 arrived, it found Leo ailing, with spasms of the chest, fever and chills. Although a doctor was summoned on April 3, with his beloved Michalina at his side and his last rites being administrated, preparing his soul for death, he quietly passed away. Within two short years, Michalina joined him. Leo and Michalina's earthly remains are buried at Roseland Cemetery, but their spirits can be found at the old St. Margarita's Catholic Church.

The congregation outgrew and overflowed St. Margarita's some years ago, and a larger, more modern church was built. The old church now serves as the offices of the Monticello–Jefferson County Chamber of Commerce, looking the same as it did in 1915, with its impressive windows. In the turn of the last century, stained-glassed windows were installed in churches for the primary purpose of not allowing those within a building to see the world outside. An original church pew can also be found in the old building.

The chamber of commerce staff and visitors alike have experienced many ghostly encounters, from cabinet doors opening and closing by themselves to objects left in one place and relocated by unseen hands elsewhere, heavy footsteps heard on the old hardwood floors and a sudden and unexpected chill that engulfs the two-room building, sending shivers up and down the spine. Ghosts tend to make their presences known to all kinds of visitors. They do not have a preference regarding those who believe in them or not. It only takes one encounter to realize that ghosts do exist.

Mary Frances Gambling, retired executive director of the Monticello–Jefferson County Chamber of Commerce, stated in an interview that she "found it quite interesting working in a haunted building, but at times it did get unnerving hearing doors opening and closing knowing I was the only one, or only 'live one,' in the building." She also said that "it became annoying at times when I would be unable to find an object on my desk and later find it sitting on a counter or table in the back of the building" and has verbally chastised the ghosts for taking her off task.

Many of the townsfolk have been witness to another, ghostly phenomenon while out for their evening strolls, walking past the old church. The ethereal sounds of organ music can often be heard coming from the locked and empty building. It is believed that if this is the place Leo chose to spend much of his afterlife, as he did in his lifetime, and with Michalina being St. Margarita's organist, perhaps she followed suit to stay near her soul mate. Perhaps she chose to return to the one place that Leo loved the most.

Visitors have been known to capture a photo depicting paranormal activity, and a video camera on a tripod taping a presentation recorded the sound of organ music.

Ghosts often choose to return in their afterlives to a place of peace, love and contentment that they enjoyed and experienced during their lifetimes. This place of familiarity is indeed a venue for a haunting. A high amount of emotional content still lingers in old churches.

The Majewskis, having been kind and caring folks, always there to lend a helping hand, who is to say that these ghostly encounters couldn't be another way of them continuing this practice by letting the community have some confirmation that death is not the end. Our spirits, the essence of who we were, live on and soar.

MERCHANT DENHAM AND HIS CUPOLA

It must have seemed like another world in 1832 when, at the age of fourteen, John arrived in his new country and his new town of Monticello, Florida. He came from the village of Dunbar, Scotland, taking months to arrive as the slow-going sailing vessel would stop at each port to deliver its weary passengers.

John's father, Andrew, and mother, Jane, packed their worldly possessions and their large brood of lads and lassies and joined other Scots who had arrived in the New World seeking their fortunes. Risking the terrors of the deep, and the uncertainties of an unknown country, they landed in what is now Baltimore, Maryland. From there they continued their journey. Eventually arriving in Monticello, they proceeded to make it their new home, a place in which young John would grow old and prosperous and eventually die.

John, being from hardy stock, was not afraid of working hard, and his work paid off. He went into the export and import business, becoming a master at his craft. Shipping goods to foreign ports on cargo ships down the St. Marks River, John was a commanding man whose boisterous voice could often be heard from some distance away.

When the Civil War arrived, many businesses were forced to close due to the poor economic conditions. However, John Denham continued in the supply trade, but for the benefit of the Southern army, gathering in the country's products to sustain the fighting soldiers of the South and concentrating his efforts in assisting the Confederacy.

In 1846, John married a young lady of Scottish decent, Caroline Ellen Marvin, who had reached the age of twenty some years his junior. They became the parents of many children, several of whom died in infancy. John and Caroline's first home was located at the corner of Palmer Mill and Waukeenah Streets. As the years passed, John became a man of means and wanted to show it by building a large, spacious two-story home. The new home was built on the same street, just a few blocks away. John came by daily and watched the carpenters at their work. If he thought that they were slacking, he was quick to inform them of it.

This new home also contained an architectural oddity. The home had an impressive cupola on its top. These small structures were built on homes primarily before the Civil War, letting the master of the house get to the highest vantage point to watch his field hands work. They were also built on homes on the sea coast so that the mistress of the house

Mr. Denham can be seen in his cupola on moonlit nights staring down upon Monticello.

could look out and see if she could spot the ship of the man of the house coming in from the sea.

John built his cupola so that he could get to the highest vantage point and see what his neighbors were doing, as well as their material possessions. John wanted the best of everything and would observe his neighbors. If they purchased an item of worth, John would go out and purchase one better. As the evening sun set, John could be seen climbing the small spiral staircase carrying a lantern and sitting on his perch in the cupola.

John was known to be quarrelsome and, at times, was known to shoot off his rifle just to get his neighbors' attention or to flaunt his possessions.

John died at the age of sixty-six in 1874 at his home, but even today he can still be seen up in his cupola. John has often been seen making an appearance during the historic Monticello ghost tours. It is common for guests or the local neighborhood folks out for an evenings stroll to look up and see the imposing figure of a man in the cupola.

Ghosts tend to be lodged in places that once were theirs, and they consider these places to have either painful or happy memories. It appears as though ghosts just want to be acknowledged or tell a story. John lived a very interesting life, being active until the end; perhaps he still has something more to say or is just continuing to draw attention to himself.

Everyone who has an interest in ghost hunting—or perhaps just wants to be frightened or see if ghosts really do exist—tends to visit places that are haunted because they know that they may be able to catch a glimpse of a ghost on film or on audiotape. A ghost hunter is well aware of the fact that a ghost will make movements because it is upset about something or because it just wants to make its presence known.

Ghosts enjoy being around people because they can draw energy from their cellphones, cameras and so on. Guests seem to have a problem keeping their electrical gadgets charged. A ghost can only get stronger if there is energy present that allows it to become strong enough to materialize.

Most ghosts tend to make their presences known as the way they were before they died. They want people to see them as who they once were, and they tend to hold on to past memories. Many ghosts can materialize in physical form, as bright balls of light thought to be energy or in a misty, smoky form known as ectoplasmic mist.

John's house sat empty for a few years, and many of the townspeople reported that they would hear the sound of music and chattering of voices, as if some ghostly gathering was occurring in the lower-right first-floor parlor. The home presently, serving as the John Denham Bed-and-Breakfast, was voted by *USA Today* in 2003 as the third most haunted bed-and-breakfast in the entire country. A host of ghostly activity occurs in the old historic house, with guests often arriving at the bed-and-breakfast as skeptics and leaving much enlightened about the world of ghosts.

John is not the only ghost that haunts the bed-and-breakfast. The house plays host to at least two ghosts. A lovely, lonely ghost affectionately known as "Aunt Sarah" has also made herself known on numerous occasions—including allowing guests from time to time to capture her in a photo.

Aunt Sarah was always the bridesmaid and never the bride; she reportedly was once left at the altar. But it was rumored that Aunt Sarah was known to keep company with a well-known and much-married politician and that they would secretly meet up in her room for afternoon trysts. Apparently, from time to time, they are still meeting. Guests who have small children have told stories of them being tucked into their bed covers by gentle, unseen hands. Other guests have reported lights going on and off at night, the rocking chair in the blue room rocking by itself and televisions being turn on by unseen hands.

The inn's resident pet dogs often seemingly see and interact with someone or something that guests and the innkeeper cannot see. There is also a lady in white, similar to an old-fashioned bridal grown, that has been seen scurrying across the yard; whether Aunt Sarah or another ghost entirely, she is quite a spectral sight to see.

If you want to stay in an authentic haunted bed-and-breakfast, this one is highly recommended. Your next ghostly encounter awaits you.

FLORIDA'S FIRST BRICK SCHOOLHOUSE

Old schoolhouses have been known to have a reputation for being haunted. The old Jefferson Academy is no exception.

Jefferson Academy was built on the site of Monticello's first schoolhouse, a small two-room structure erected shortly after Monticello was established as the county seat in 1827. About the time Florida received statehood in 1845, a growth spurt occurred in Monticello, with many new families calling Monticello home. The need for a bigger school building was a must—with an enrollment of about one hundred students, the little schoolhouse was bursting. With the combined efforts of the community and its many fundraisers—such as New England boil dinners, box socials and handicraft bazaars, culminating with the donation of funds from a Freemason organization—the construction on the new Jefferson Academy was ready to begin.

In early 1851, bricks kilned on a local plantation were brought to the site by ox cart. Master builder Samuel Carroll and his slaves, whom he had educated in his craft, worked diligently on the academy's construction. The new Jefferson Academy was completed in March 1852. The two-story building was sixty feet by fifty-five and historically was the first brick school building in the entire state of Florida. The well-constructed and massive (for the times) school building became envied throughout the state.

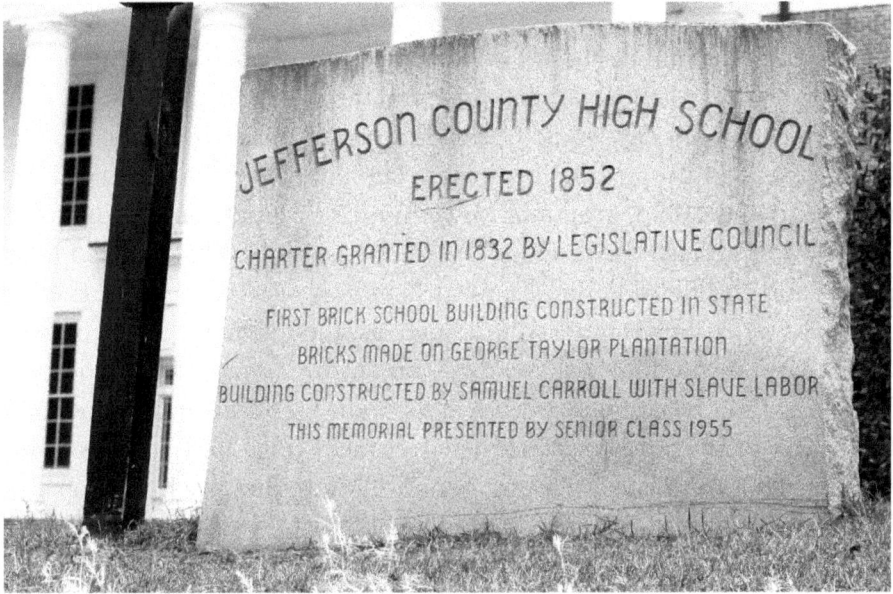

The voices and laughter of long-ago students still fill this historic old school, built in 1852.

Shortly after its completion, a dedication of the new academy was held, and a barbecue was enjoyed by all who attended. The town and country folks came for the celebration of the new school, which was a striking and imposing structure and the pride of all Jefferson County.

The school year was forty-six weeks long, with each term being eleven and a half weeks. During an era before public schools were designed to be free in Florida, students who attended the academy were required to pay tuition. Students attending the primary grades first through eighth were required to pay five dollars per quarter. Students in grades ninth through twelfth paid ten dollars per quarter, with an additional two-dollar fee if the students took a language class. Students were expected to furnish their own supplies, including books, writing slates and chalk.

The academy's first teachers were local ministers and men in the community with higher education. Their salaries were set at twenty-five dollars per month. At this time and place, male teachers were the norm. Teachers were expected to be virtuous and have extremely high morals. They were also expected to keep the schoolhouse clean, draw each day's water supply from the school's well and keep the wood stove fired up on cold days. The students' families provided the wood for the fires.

A typical school day would begin with a patriotic song, a salute to the flag and a scripture reading or prayer. The main subjects were spelling, reading, penmanship, grammar, vocal music, arithmetic and geography. There were no tests as we know them today. Students memorized long poems and had figuring races, and spelling bees were often social events.

Recess and lunch time were short, as the primary focus of the academy were the four Rs ("reading, riting, rithmetic and recitations"). During a time before playground equipment existed, various students' fathers or older brothers constructed crude swings and seesaws. The younger children played popular games of the times, such as drop the handkerchief, hide-and-seek, blindman's bluff. Older students enjoyed games such as dodge ball and red rover.

Discipline was strict at the academy: children were made to stand in line and march to and from their desk. The students were expected to stand in front of the teacher to recite readings. Punishment was often dealt out in the form of a ruler to the palm of the hand. Students who did not do their assigned work were made to sit in a corner and wear a dunce cap. Standing with one's nose inside a circle drawn on the blackboard was another common punishment. In extreme cases of bad behavior, a whipping was administered with a leather strip.

The mainstay of Jefferson County economy at the time was farming, and many of the students had to stay home in the spring to help plant and plow, and they would likewise help harvest in the fall. The older boys often didn't go to school in the summer because of farm work. During this time, their educational needs were the responsibility of the mother of the house. After a long day working in the fields, the boys would then be required to devote one to two hours each evening after the supper meal to their studies.

In the early 1860s, with the arrival of the Civil War (or the war of Northern Aggression, as Monticello's men folk referred to it), the academy's first female teachers were hired. Ella Rhodes and Elizabeth McCants were both married women and of sound mind and morals who began teaching at the academy when many of the male teachers adhered to the cause and joined the war effort. Both women had previously taught in private schools.

After the war, veteran Colonel William O. Girardeau, a man of higher education and a mathematician, became principal of the academy. A strict man with a no-nonsense approach, the Colonel (as he was simply known) knew the value of an education and worked hard to instill this in his charges. He valued honesty and order among the students and struggled to keep control of the school; he was constantly engaged in a battle against its inadequate resources.

With the passage of time, the once pretentious academy building became inadequate for the needs of an increased student attendance, as well as for the new mandated school requirements concerning equipment, staff, sanitation and curriculum. Newer, more modern schools were built fitted to the needs of an increased enrollment and of educational progress.

The once stately structure sits quietly now, as if a gentle giant has been stifled. It is bare of all human inhabitants. However, the spirits of its former teachers and students fill the building like fans fill an arena at a sporting event.

Strange tales surround this grand old building that is steeped in history; it is swamped with stories about the laughter and merrymaking sounds

The first brick schoolhouse in the state of Florida.

of glee from ghostly children from long ago who once called this place their school. Precious moments of childhood have been imbedded into the building's environment.

In recent years, the building has gone through a series of repairs. During one such episode, a construction foreman was living in a small, portable mobile home in front of the academy. More than once he was awoken during the middle of the night by the sound of children's squeals of laughter. The foreman, thinking that he had left the building's door unlocked and that a group of local children had entered the building and were vandalizing it, immediately got up and checked. The minute he turned the door's ancient lock, the racket stopped, he reported. After each encounter, making a thorough check of the building, he would then return to his slumber, locking the door behind him.

Other ghostly phenomena has included the frequent occurrence of a bright ball of light seen bouncing from window to window on the second floor in the rear of the building and the unidentified rapping sound coming from a first-floor classroom. After much thought—and with the building being repeatedly checked for the sound's origins, and finding no natural source for the sound—it is believed that perhaps it is the sound of a ghostly old schoolmarm rapping on her desk with her ruler, trying to bring her unruly class to order. Imagine being in school for more than one hundred years!

PALMER HOUSE

THE DOCTOR IS IN

The Palmer House was built in the mid-1800s and remained in the Palmer family for many years. It was bequeathed to John Dabney Palmer, a fifth-generation doctor in this family. Dr. Palmer was a graduate of medicine and an author of several books on chemistry, some of which are still in print today. He also fought by his father's side in the Civil War. He married a beautiful woman named Laura Willie, who bore him a son, allowing the family name to continue another generation. By 1880, the Palmer household also included his widowed mother and a lovely young eighteen-year-old black woman named Lilla Prince.

The Palmer House Antiques Shop now occupies the home and experiences an abundance of ghostly activity, including the frequent materialization of apparitions; drapes being pulled aside by unseen hands; visitors often being touched; unexplained noises, including loud thumps, screams and knocks; and the general feeling of dread and a heaviness in the chest.

As was common in that era, the doctor was often the undertaker as well. It has been reported that Dr. Palmer did also dabble in this field. In those times, the home would often house both the doctor's office and the mortuary. Both were true for Dr. Palmer. His mortuary was on the second floor of the family home, and his office was a separate building set in the corner of his front yard.

Though a brilliant physician and scientist, even by twenty-first-century standards Dr. Palmer would have been considered unorthodox. As a

The Palmer House, Monticello's most haunted structure.

The office of Dr. J. Dabney Palmer, located in the front yard.

mortician, Dr. Palmer had a personal quirk in believing that the deceased should be buried with their blood. He had a gentleman of color who worked for him whom the local folks referred to as "Poltergeist," due to the report that he did not cast a shadow. Poltergeist drove a buckboard pulled by mules. The following was the procedure when Dr. Palmer had a body in his mortuary and was getting ready for burial: Poltergeist would go to the cemetery and dig the grave, and then he would return to Dr. Palmer. By that time, Dr. Palmer would have extracted the blood from the deceased and put it in a container, which would be given to Poltergeist, who would return to the cemetery and empty the blood-filled container into the grave. Shortly thereafter, the body would be interred.

This is the room that housed Dr. Palmer's mortuary.

One day, a fierce argument broke out between Poltergeist and Dr. Palmer as the doctor was handing a blood-filled container to him. The origin of the argument is unknown, but it is the reason why the Palmer House is known as the most haunted house in Monticello. Poltergeist took the container and threw it and its contents, which landed on Dr. Palmer, the wall and the deceased. Through the years, other owners have tried to remove the bloodstain from the wall, to no avail. The wall has been scrubbed, painted, kilz stained and wallpapered, but no matter how much time has passed or how many coats of paint were applied, the stain returned. The current owner purchased the home to be used as an antiques shop. Before opening the shop, in making a few renovations, the owner removed the bloodstained wall from the upstairs room directly above the fireplace in the lower-left-side parlor.

As opening day for the Palmer Antiques House approached, the owner stocked the shop with an array of lovely antiques, including a large framed portrait that she hung above the fireplace in the parlor that is directly underneath the room where the bloodstained wall was removed.

After a short while, a patron came in and wanted to purchase the portrait above the fireplace. The owner reported that as the portrait was removed from the wall she almost fainted. The bloodstain pattern that was on the wall that had been removed from the room one floor above had returned and was now above the fireplace! Even today you can visit the antiques shop and bear witness to the bloodstained wall.

A small building that faces south can be seen adjacent to the historic Palmer House. The one-room building is no bigger than a typical storage shed or one-car garage in today's standards. However, back in the day when Dr. Dabney Palmer served as primary physician for the Monticello area, it was utilized, rather practically, as his office.

The office usually consisted of nothing more than a waiting room and an examination room. Some offices had the waiting room and the examination room separate from each other. However, it was often the case that the two rooms were combined. The design of the office actually had no practicality or efficiency whatsoever, and patients would often complain about the lack of privacy in having to be examined in front of one another. The interior of the offices typically consisted of the doctor's desk and an examination table and appeared rather drab and sterile, cluttered with instruments, bottles, prescription pads and books. There were typically a few chairs in the waiting area for patients, as well as a spittoon, of course, which was a necessity in the days of tobacco chewers. It was also proper and common for doctors of this time to display their microscopes, diplomas, pictures of professional friends and teachers and anything else associated with the medical field or their career. Despite advice against it, doctors also often displayed objects such as skeletons and anatomical specimens in plain view, because it demonstrated their knowledge of medicine and anatomy.

Medicine during most of the 1800s was practiced in private homes or, occasionally, in a private doctor's office. Most doctors traveled by horseback or by foot. Considering this, and the fact that he only had access to those items that could fit in his hand-held doctor's bag or saddlebags, a doctor was limited in the instruments and medications that were available to him. Due to the combination of this and the expectation of the doctor to treat a wide variety of ailments, it is no wonder, then, that the quality of care may have been lacking. Many times patients were examined and treated in their own homes. Examinations consisted of a thorough checkup of the patient's body, which could have included the use of a stethoscope to listen to the patient's chest, lungs and bowels, as well as a blood or urine analysis. A common treatment for many ailments was known as "bleeding." The theory behind this was that illnesses and diseases were carried in the blood. Therefore, by repeatedly ridding the body of blood, the patient could be cured. A single bloodletting could draw as much as twelve ounces of blood, which is about equal to 6 percent of an adult's total blood volume.

Other common treatments included dietary restrictions, rest, bathing remedies, massage, blistering, sweating, enemas, purging through the use of diuretics and emetics like syrup of ipecac, prescriptions, creams and herbal pills.

Dr. Palmer also owned the Monticello Drug Company, as back in his day he was considered an apothecary. An apothecary was much like a present-day pharmacist and doctor all rolled into one. The medical professional would generally have a shop where people would visit and explain what ailed them. The apothecary would then dispense medicines, ointments and tinctures, many of which he would formulate on his own, to treat the symptoms. Other general medical advice was given, and sometimes the apothecary would suggest surgery, midwifery and other services that would later be preformed by a specialist. Upon entering the shop, one would see rows and rows of bottles displayed behind the counter, each filled with an herb or medicine. These glass bottles were usually clear, with a simple stopper on top.

It is speculated that Dr. Palmer invented the famous Elixir 666 at the apothecary. This compound had a high concentration of quinine within its ingredients and was the best-selling remedy for malaria during a time when many of the townsfolk were afflicted with the disease. The years passed, and old age began to creep up on Dr. Palmer. In 1897, a brilliant young pharmacist by the name of Spencer Tharp Roberts arrived in Monticello from nearby Valdosta, Georgia. Spencer developed a close personal and business relationship with Dr. Palmer and his wife, Laura, who assisted him as a druggist clerk at the apothecary. Spencer later moved in with the Palmers and became their boarder. Shortly thereafter, he purchased the Monticello Drug Company. In 1909, Dr. Palmer passed from this earthly realm, having never obtained a patent on his elixir. It was common for many druggists and physicians to never have their concoctions patented, mostly to avoid having to divulge during the patenting process the often hazardous and questionable ingredients.

About the time Dr. Palmer died, young pharmacist Roberts incorporated the Monticello Drug Company, forming Monticello Drugs, and had Elixir 666 patented under the name Roberts Remedies No. 666. Many wonder where the number "666" came from. Was it something devilish? Some old-timers say that it tasted like the devil. The truth was that it was sent to the patent office on prescription log no. 666.

On some late, moonlit nights, passersby have experienced rather odd occurrences. As it has been told, a frock-coated gentleman wearing what appears to be a top hat, as was often worn by astute men of the time, has been seen scurrying from the office and into the home of Dr. Palmer, carrying what one would think of when describing an old doctor's bag. Could it be Dr. Palmer, still hurrying off after all these years to make his rounds, or perhaps Dr. Palmer can't rest in peace because his name is not on the 666 elixir patent.

JEFFERSON COUNTY COURTHOUSE

O ld courthouses are known to be haunted, and the Jefferson County Courthouse is no exception.

Courtrooms are a traditional place of judgment; could they also be places of final judgment? For the believers who feel that the spirits of the dead can linger on among the living, locations historically associated with the law present a prolific ground for ghostly hauntings. After all, in the mortal world, the law affects people in poignant, life-changing ways—even ending the lives of some. This connection may remain strong even in death.

Standing in the middle of U.S. Highway 19 and U.S. Highway 90 in the center of town, the courthouse is Monticello's most notable landmark, built in the typical style of the early 1900 county courthouses that can be found in most every small southern town. County courthouses were said to be built as large, elaborate structures so that the different counties could not brag about relative magnificence when every county had one! These old buildings reflected community pride.

One of the prime reasons for building such massive, sturdy courthouses was to have a fireproof place for storing important county records. Another reason was to provide large courtrooms; in the early days, the public eagerly attended trials. When important court proceedings would

The courthouse is the scene of a ghostly shooting that plays out on the anniversary of the event. Built in 1909 in a style typical of most southern courthouses, its entrance faces U.S. Highway 90.

be heard, with the general public attending, one could fine hot dog, lemonade and roasted peanut hawkers stationed out in front, eagerly waiting to sell their goods when the court would take a recess and to find out the news from inside the courtroom.

Women were the primary audience that attended trials, perhaps to escape the mundane day-to-day life of an everyday housewife. Until 1949, Florida women were subject to an absolute exclusion from jury service.

Courthouses were also the official timekeepers. Most had prominent clocks on them, as few people had wristwatches in the early days. Courthouses also housed the public restrooms for downtown shoppers and others doing business in town. In addition, they provided public meeting places.

The present-day courthouse built in 1909 was the third courthouse built at this location, the first being a log cabin, followed by a more permanent structure built in 1841. The courthouse of 1841 was built of wood and measured about fifty feet square. It had two stories and was of plain and dignified design. A hall and six rooms, used for offices and jury rooms, occupied the lower story, while the upper floor was entirely devoted to the courtroom. A veranda extended across the front of the building at second-story height and was reached by a broad stairway ascending from the ground, affording the only means of access to the courtroom. Running beneath the stairway and entirely across the building's front was a terrace equal in width to the veranda above it. In later years, champion chess players would gather and engage in friendly games while enjoying the cool shade of the beautiful surrounding live-oaks, which in later years were sacrificed to the needs of the present courthouse, except for one great tree to the south (the Old Hanging Tree) that still spreads its arms above passing traffic today.

During this time, court was only conducted twice a year, in spring and fall terms. One of the most unusual laws on the Jefferson County books at the time was that when each prospective bridegroom obtained a marriage license, he was required to sign a pledge worthy note. The prospective bridegroom was required to have one or two friends sign with him, and the two or three men assumed a $2,000 bond to the governor of the territory to fulfill the conditions of the marriage contract. Failure to do this meant incurring the stated penalty and thus render the bond null and void, which from all evidence seems to have been seldom carried out. This law later would be called "breach of promise."

The courthouse built in 1841 had a bell tower. Not known to have had ghostly activity, it did see its share of excitement. At a time when telephones and mobile radios had not been invented, the bell in the courthouse tower served as a warning system for residents. A watchman was employed and would ring the bell to alert citizens in the event of a fire, a major news event or of some impending natural disaster. On one particularly hot and humid late summer night, the bell proved too much a temptation for some young boys looking for some excitement. When the watchman left his post to take care of a call from nature, the boys tied a calf to the bell tower rope. When it began to squirm, ringing the bell excessively, they hid in nearby bushes to watch the excitement as half the townsfolk, dressed in nightclothes, rushed to the courthouse square to see what was happening.

The courthouse bells would also be rung when a trial jury had returned with a verdict so that the public, lawyers and judges could be called back to hear it.

The present courthouse has had its share of excitement as well. On election night in 1934, with communication not being what it is today, the townsfolk, in traditional southern style, gathered at the county courthouse to await election returns. As midnight approached, there was a heated exchange of words between two local men, Claude Gifford and Saunders Sauls. First it was verbal insults, but soon it became physical with a slap and a push and a shove. To the gathered crowd's horrific surprise, guns were drawn, raised and fired, with the men shooting each other to death as the onlookers scattered. Both men lay dead, with a bystander injured.

This senseless, tragic event occurred at the front paved entrance of the courthouse. Through the ensuing years, from time to time a residual haunting of this traumatic occurrence can be witnessed. A residual haunting is a playback of a past event. The apparitions involved are not spirits but rather are "recordings" of the event. These occurrences often replay themselves on the anniversary. Some say that it is "penance" the killers must do in order for them to cross over; others believe that the spirits do not even know that they are dead. Whatever the case, for those who had the fortunate or unfortunate opportunity to witness the haunting, it was forever etched in their minds.

Another ghostly phenomenon that occurs in this historic old building is the sound of a gavel hitting the podium in the second-floor courtroom. Courthouse employees working late and often alone, as well as the building maintenance and cleaning crews, all have the same story to tell. Could this be a ghostly judge still conducting court?

Jefferson County's founding fathers and early citizens enjoyed the good times and took the bad times in stride, always doing their best to keep a sense of humor. All one has to do is look above the front entrance of the courthouse. There for all to see are the words "SUUM CUIQUE" ("Sue Um Quick"?). In Latin, its meaning translates as "To each his own." How befitting to be over the door of a courthouse. What were they thinking? Were they fans of poet Ralph Waldo Emerson and his 1841 poem "Suum Cuique," or did they want to leave future generations wondering?

YE OLE HANGING TREE

A passerby or newcomer arriving into the heart of Monticello will see a majestic oak tree known as the Old Hanging Tree or the Meeting Oak. The tree is said to be more than 250 years old, with its branches stretching up toward the sky against the backdrop of the town's historic courthouse.

In the Old World, there was a time when kings meted out justice from under an old oak tree. History tells that most American towns had an oak tree by their courthouse from which they delivered their own style of justice—at the end of a long rope. In Monticello, Thursday was designated as hanging day. If there were any criminals found guilty of crimes punishable by death, they were taken up to the hanging tree on Thursday afternoon. All of the shops and local business would close at noon, and people would make a day of it, packing a lunch and bringing the family to witness the town's swift justice. Even to this day, if you travel through town on a Thursday afternoon, you are likely to find that most shops and businesses are closed up, as traditions in small southern towns are slow to change.

Before 1923, hanging was still the primary mode of execution in the state of Florida. The last hangings in Jefferson County were held on January 13, 1911. The unfortunate men who were given this

The Old Hanging Tree is a reminder of times passed, when justice in Monticello was simple and swift.

distinction were arrested and found guilty by a jury of their peers and sentenced to death. Joseph Curry and Sam Newkirk were both hanged in Monticello for a Jefferson County murder. The pair murdered local resident Jim Horton, who was beaten and killed with a wooden club on October 15, 1910.

The rope that was used for a hanging was usually made of hemp and at least 0.75 inches and not more than 1.25 inches in diameter, as well as about thirty feet in length. It would be soaked and stretched the night before to eliminate stiffness, spring or coiling. The hangman's knot was then treated with soap, wax or oil so that the rope would slide easily through the knot. If careful measuring and planning were not done, strangulation, obstructed blood flow or beheading could result. The noose needed to be placed snugly around the person's neck, behind their left ear, which would cause the neck to break. If properly done, death would be caused by dislocation of the third and fourth vertebrae or by asphyxiation (cutting off the flow of oxygen rather than the flow of blood).

There are four methods of hanging that could be employed. The short drop, which was the preferred method before 1850, was performed by placing the person on the back of a cart, horse or other vehicle, with the noose around their neck. When the object was moved, the person was left dangling from the rope. The person then died of strangulation, which may have taken between ten and twenty minutes. Another common implement used in the short drop was the ladder: the condemned would climb to the top, and then the ladder would be pulled away or turned. This is where the slang phrase term for hanging "to be turned off" comes from.

Similar to the short drop was the suspension method. It also caused death by using the weight of the body to tighten the trachea with the noose. There was very little to no struggle before the person would go limp. This was due to the reduction of blood flow to the brain.

The next is the standard drop, which came into use about 1866. It consists of a drop of between four and six feet. It was much more humane than the short drop because it was supposed to break the victim's neck, causing immediate paralysis and unconsciousness.

Last was the long drop, the method that was introduced about 1872 as advancement to the standard drop. Instead of every person falling the same distance, the person's height and weight were used to determine how much slack would be provided in the rope so that the neck would be broken but not so much that the person was decapitated. The neck would be jerked back rapidly, and the neck would break predictably.

During the Civil War, the tree became known as the Meeting Oak. It was the spot where our brave young men in gray met to receive their orders and find out the location of their next duty. This was also where many families gathered to say their last goodbyes to their loved ones before they headed off to fight in the war. For many, it would be the last time they would ever see them. Even today, you can see a large yellow ribbon tied around the old oak, proof that Monticello is rich in historical tradition and that it has always been proud of its men and women who serve and is eager for their safe and swift return.

Maggie Thompson wrote in her journal:

> *I stood there looking at him under that old oak tree its braches shading us from the suns relentless assault. I stood there trying not to cry as I looked at Jacob. Little Sally clung to him crying please Daddy don't go. I choked back those tears trying not to let my husband see my fear. As we kissed and said our goodbyes all I could think of was my God this may be the last time I see him. As soon as he turned to leave I picked up Sally and we both sobbed uncontrollably.*

Jacob Thompson would not return home to his family, like so many others who went way to fight.

It is not uncommon for folks taking pictures on the historic Monticello ghost tour to capture various photographic anomalies and strange images when photographing the old tree. If you closely inspect the tree, you'll notice scars from where the old tree has been struck by cars. Many a motorist traveling the road at night has claimed to see the phantom of a Confederate soldier under the tree in his crisp gray uniform, weapon glistening in the moonlight. Now, if you happen to be traveling through town on a moonlit night, and you happen across the ghost of an old Civil War soldier under the Old Hanging Tree, drive carefully. If you should find yourself in an accident and you tell Monticello's finest the tale of your ghostly encounter, you can bet that it won't be the first time they have heard the story. Just be prepared for them to question your sobriety.

MR. PERKINS AND HIS OPERA HOUSE

In 1890, an enterprising, self-made Monticello businessman named John Henry Perkins—his roots deep in the Jefferson County soil, the epitome of a southern gentleman, with a love of the theater—built his opera house.

A man of means, he was afforded the opportunity to travel to and fro to see live theatrical performances. He and his wife, India, often traveled to the Springer Opera House in Columbus, Georgia, billed to be the finest opera house between Washington D.C. and New Orleans. The 350-mile round trip consisted of a horse and carriage, train and walking and would be a two- to three-day affair.

Mr. Perkins purchased a large city block of property near the county courthouse some time earlier—with the news from an old acquaintance, Henry Plant, who had recently purchased the old Atlantic & Gulf Railroad and had established the Savannah, Florida & Western Railroad. Plant, without much persuasion, agreed to build a Monticello station, with its trains running into Monticello from south Georgia and beyond.

The tourist boom was emerging with the constructing of the elegant St. Elmo's Hotel, and with the new train service, wealthy northerners were arriving to winter at the hotel, enjoying the mild temperatures and escaping the harsh winters of the North.

Mr. Perkins was an astute businessman and knew that the timing was right to fulfill a secret desire to build his own opera house. He had always wanted

The Monticello Opera House, one of the town's most notable buildings and the home of the dancing ghost.

to be able to share his love of the live theater with his friends and neighbors, and now he could. He would build a two-story brick building large enough to be serviceable to him for his other business interests, to include a general store, a sewing machine shop and a hardware store that would also sell farm implements. The second story of his opera house would include the theater, which some say has unparalleled acoustics and the largest stage in the area.

The Perkins Block, as it would come to be known, was completed midyear in 1890. Mr. Perkins was forty-five years old. With the northern tourists still in town, it was a grand time to be in Monticello. With the trains running into Monticello, the area folks would travel to Monticello on Friday afternoons and stay at the grand old St. Elmo's Hotel one block east of the opera house and attend its performances.

For the next thirty-seven years, the opera house's playbill would included both professional touring groups, local productions, operas, minstrel shows and Shakespearean productions. Week after week, it seemed that each performance was better than the last one. Mr. Perkins himself was considered to be somewhat musical and often could be found "warming" up the audiences with a song or two played out on the orchestra's piano.

The opera house was a mainstay in Monticello and even today is one of Monticello's most identifiable buildings.

In the early summer of 1927, Mr. Perkins found himself despondent and grief stricken; he had lost his only child, a daughter named Mary, and in the spring his darling wife India had also departed from this earth. As he stood and stared into the mirror, he hardly recognized the face looking back at him. The years had gone by too quickly, and he was no longer the handsome, dapper and energetic man he had once been. Mr. Perkins was eighty-two years old, and due to a fall that injured his hip, he was forced to walk with a cane. He no longer could waltz with the music of Strauss, and his arthritic fingers kept him from playing the piano.

In August of the same year, this already sad and broken man was dealt another blow. In 1889, the railroad changed hands following the death of Henry Plant, and the town leaders and businessmen had never developed more than a cordial relationship with its new owners. The ongoing dispute with the railroad escalated in late August, and in an act of defiance, with a rumble brewing between townsfolk and the railroad, late one night railroad men sneaked in, unbeknownst to the sleeping town, and removed the tracks coming into and going out of Monticello, thus rerouting the railroad.

With transportation not being like it is today, attendance quickly dwindled at the opera house; in late fall, Mr. Perkins was forced to close its doors. In December, Mr. Perkins died suddenly, some say of a broken heart. Although his earthly remains were interred at Roseland Cemetery, his spirit is still very much in his opera house.

The opera house set silent, and tales of an old ghost light abounded. Mr. Perkins, it seems, being the practical gentleman he was, believed in the superstition of the "ghost light," which often could be found in old theaters. It simply was a single bare lamp left burning in the middle of the stage all night. Mr. Perkins had a reputation of being agreeable, but he was adamant that the lamp be left on nightly. It was believed that if the light was left on you avoided the bad luck or sadness of a theater being left "dark" (with no shows running due to lack of money or unsuccessful productions). But then again, theater folk are usually a superstitious bunch, and considering the amount of things that can go wrong in a live performance, I guess an ounce of prevention is worth a pound of cure.

Mr. Perkins always made sure that the light was left on. Even in his afterlife, while his spirit soars in his opera house, he has kept the ghost light burning.

Concerning another tradition many old theaters practiced, and one in which Mr. Perkins followed suit, it was thought that if you closed the theater once a week it gave ghosts the opportunity to perform onstage to appease them and prevent them from cursing the theater or sabotaging the set or production. Many theater ghosts are thought to be former actors.

Even in the early days of live theater, it was customary and considered good luck to give the director and the leading lady, after closing night, a bouquet of flowers. Back in Mr. Perkins's day, the flowers were thought to have to come from the graveyard. Graveyard flowers were given on closing night to symbolize the death of the show.

Mr. Perkins's opera house sat idle for many years, its spiral staircase was removed, with plaster falling from the once ornate walls and ceiling and its roof leaking. There was much talk about having the building demolished. Then, out of the blue in 1972, a small group was formed with its only mission being to save the Perkins Opera House, and save it the members did, eventually bringing it back to its "glory days."

Mr. Perkins often tries to show how appreciative he is to have his building restored and once again filled full of patrons enjoying a variety of performances. He has been known now and again to join them on stage. The opera house staff through the years have had a variety of encounters with him. The former curator had a regular habit: the first thing she said as she arrived was, "Good morning Mr. Perkins," and the last thing as she locked the door at the end of the day would be to say, "Good night Mr. Perkins."

A host of paranormal occurrences have been witnessed through the years, from an apparition of Mr. Perkins interacting with young people and chaperones when the opera house hosted the high school prom to objects being moved and reappearing else where and the piano that's stationed on the stage playing a few notes now and again by an unseen musician.

Mr. Perkins decided to return and remain in his afterlife to the one place he loved the most, the place where much emotional energy was spent—laughter, merrymaking, music, dancing, actors and actresses. Mr. Perkins is in his element once again.

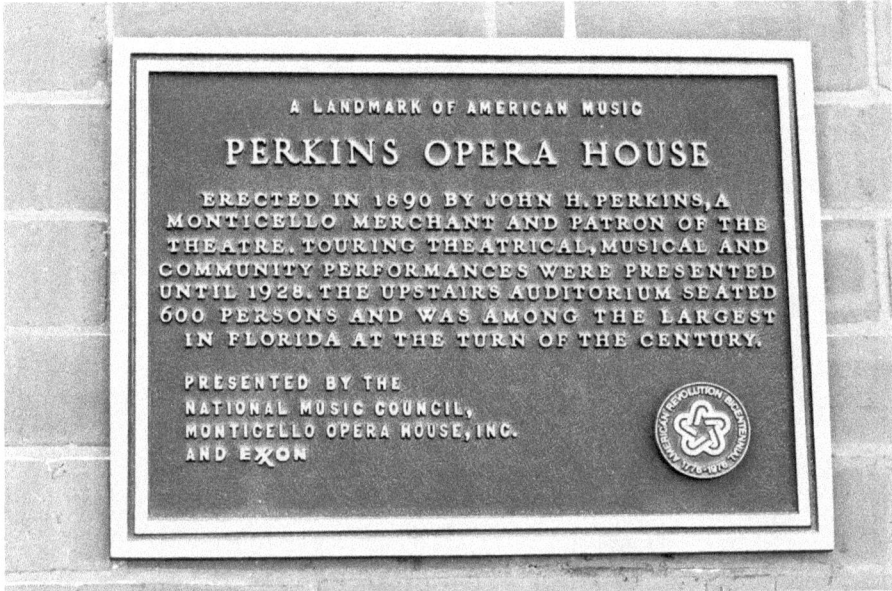

Built in 1890, old opera houses are known venues for hauntings.

Tales of haunted theaters and opera houses abound. Almost every theater, in fact, has unexplainable occurrences that some attribute to ghosts.

The Big Bend Ghost Trackers team, professional paranormal investigators, has conducted two successful investigations here, one interacting with Mr. Perkins, having him oblige a request, as well as videotaping Mr. Perkins dancing with one of the team members. Evidence of paranormal activity has been captured on video, audio, still photography and by the naked eye. In 2004, the opera house was authenticated to be a true haunted location.

It is also believed that there might be an additional ghost or two that haunts the opera house. Some time in the 1940s, a black gentleman was working on the furnace that exploded, burning him to death.

As a historical note, furniture refurbisher Homer Formsby got his start in the opera house. One of Monticello's native sons, he rented a small basement room and opened a cabinet shop. During the time Homer lived in Monticello, the tung oil tree was very prevalent, and there were many tung oil orchards. Homer discovered that he could extract oil from the trees and used it as a primary ingredient in his famous furniture polish.

A DEDICATED BLACKSMITH STILL AT WORK

In every American town from the 1800s to the early 1900s, one would expect to find livery stables, feed stores, wagon shops, blacksmith shops, horse corrals and horse traders in about the same ratio that we now find auto dealers, repair shops, parts stores and fueling stations. This shows how much the blacksmith was a part of the local economy.

Blacksmithing was once a well-known and necessary trade in early America. Most large farms had blacksmiths to make and repair farm equipment, especially due to the remoteness of many of the farms.

The time-honored and respected blacksmithing profession dates back to biblical days: "Behold, I have created the blacksmith who blows the coals in the fire, who brings forth an instrument for his work" (Isaiah 54:16).

As times changed in America, so did the role of the blacksmith. The ability to mass-produce hammers, for example, made the blacksmith's work of producing a hammer less important. The ability of the blacksmith to make tools and parts actually helped to replace him—via his creation of tools and machines, he accomplished his work more efficiently.

In the mid-1800s, about the time of the Civil War, a blacksmith made nails, one at a time, at a rate of perhaps one per minute. Nails were expensive to purchase, and many old homesteads continued to be

The blacksmith played a crucial part of life in the early days of Monticello—shoeing horses, for one example.

built with wooden pegs. Horses, wagons and horse-drawn implements dominated the blacksmith's work.

Blacksmithing helped to develop our modern way of living. During both times of peace and war, blacksmiths have been called on to perform many tasks. Ben Franklin wrote, "For want of a nail, the shoe was lost. For want of a shoe, the horse was lost. For want of a horse, the rider was lost." In "The Village Blacksmith" (1839), Henry Wadsworth Longfellow praised the blacksmith, expressing how these craftsmen were highly revered: "His brow is wet with honest sweat, He earns whate'er he can, and looks the whole world in the face, for he owes not any man."

In early America, the village blacksmith was called on to do many things. Rumor has it that some blacksmiths even pulled teeth. Making an axe, a knife, a fireplace crane, a set of door hinges or a handful of nails were common tasks that the village smithy performed. His shop was the same as what we now know to be the local hardware store. He could also repair a log chain, put rims on wagon wheels or fix a chipped axe. Whether the village needed swords or plowshares, the blacksmith made them. The village blacksmith was basically indispensible.

In Jefferson County and Monticello, one can still find the influence of the blacksmith, most apparent in church architecture. The church building was one of the first and most important public buildings in any settlement. The churches were adorned with impressively designed architectural ironwork that can still be seen today.

Most blacksmiths were in the profession due to their fathers and grandfathers. The trade usually was generational, and they would begin their apprenticeships as young boys of age six or seven. They would usually apprentice for a period of ten years or more before setting out to start their own shop. In America, there were many opportunities for young blacksmiths.

There have been several notable blacksmiths who have resided and set up shop in Jefferson County, including Thomas Raines, whose father and grandfather were both in the trade. Thomas worked as a blacksmith shoeing horses for the Eppes Plantation before 1920, and his ancestry in Monticello dates back to its early days. Monticello's blacksmith shop sits empty today. The bellows are disconnected from the forge, long since removed.

The hammers are silent, and its fires are long since extinguished. This timeless old building was built with bricks handmade by slaves, molded from the lands rich red clay and kilned on a local plantation. The old building is one of the town's original buildings that survived the post–Civil War fires.

The building was a typical livery stable of its day, where horses, teams and wagons were held for hire and boarded in the front portion of the building, and a blacksmith shop was located in the partitioned rear. Tools of the blacksmith's trade hanged from the ceiling, with a grinding stone and wire brushes used to further smooth, brighten and polish the iron surfaces; tools of the hand, such as a hammer, anvil and chisel, were placed on workbenches. From horseshoes to wrought-iron fences for family cemetery plots, farm implements and iron frying pans, there was always plenty of work for the blacksmith and his assistant, usually an apprentice (most commonly referred to as a striker) whose job it was to swing a large sledgehammer in heavy forging operations, as directed by the blacksmith.

The building operated as a working blacksmith shop until the 1940s, when many area farmers still utilized horses in plowing and planting. But with factories emerging, times were changing, calling for mass production or replacement rather than repair. It became cheaper to replace a broken part rather than have a blacksmith repair it. The art of blacksmithing was becoming extinct. But even the dark and depressing years could not extinguish the fire blazing in a blacksmith's heart; his craft was not just the ability to earn a living wage to support his family—it was a way of life.

The blacksmith is said to still be hard at work, with the sound of his hammer heard to this very day. Here is the old smith location, one of Monticello's original buildings that survived the post–Civil War fires.

The blacksmith shop was closed and converted to accommodate various businesses many years ago. A variety of businesses that located in the old building through the years have reported the sound "akin to pennies being dropped on metal"; with old pipes and fixtures having been modernized, no source of the sounds has ever been located.

The belief is that an old blacksmith is still busy at work, smelting iron and hammering away at his workbench. In one's mind, one can imagine a sooty blacksmith hammering over a hot forge and wiping the sweat from his brow. This dedicated smith continues to work even after his earthly life has ended. Old-timers who worked as blacksmiths have all told the story about how, in the old days, when one smith would visit another, he would sometimes drop a penny into the forge so as to bugger up his welding.

In paranormal circles, based on data collected, it is a documented belief that a building's composition—construction and building materials such as bricks and sandstone—contributes to the ability of an image to imprint itself. Perhaps this centuries-old building—with its bricks built diligently with hardworking and calloused hands, each molding the bricks that would prove to pass the test of time and afford generations a chance to come to see their work and that of the dedicated blacksmith—has permanently left the residual of his many busy sunup-to-sundown days in the place he spent the majority of his time, among the living, proudly pounding out his craft.

Blacksmith's Prayer

My fire is extinct,
And my forge is decayed,
By the side of the bench
My old vise is laid.
My anvil and hammer
Lie gathering dust;
My powerful bellows
Have lost all their thrust.
My coal is now spent,
My iron's all gone,
My last nail's been driven,
And my day's work is done.

THE REVEREND AND THE COFFIN MAKER

Reverend Adam Wirick was a well-known minister of the Methodist faith. Being one of the original circuit riders, or "traveling clergy" as the Methodist referred to it, in the 1820s, the reverend was instrumental in establishing Methodism in north Florida.

Born in South Carolina in 1793, having always been a man of deep religious convictions, in about 1820 his faith brought him to St. Simons Island, Georgia, a place where John Wesley had planted the seeds of Methodism eighty years before. During the early days of Methodism, clergy did not require attendance to a seminary or biblical college; when one felt the call from God to preach, he preached.

Reverend Wirick traveled from town to town on horseback, roving over hundreds of miles, and preached more than ten thousand sermons, often in adverse conditions. This man of God kept his faith. He often slept on the damp ground or in empty, cold and dirty cabins, as well as went hungry. He was waylaid by bandits more than once, where he was left beaten and bloody. Not only did he face physical hardship, but often he endured persecution as well. Many of these traveling clergy died before their ministry careers had hardly begun. Of those who died up to 1847, nearly half were younger than thirty years old. Many were just worn out from the rigorous traveling.

Here is the home where Miss Katie Simmons fashioned her coffins. The oldest house in Monticello, it was built in 1831 and faces the busy Highway 19 North.

During one of the reverend's services, he met the lovely Catherine Edwards, fifteen years his junior. Miss Edwards was affectionately known by her middle name, Adeline. They were married in 1830 in Duval County, near the coastal Georgia boarder, and made plans to move to Monticello.

The district superintendent and overseer of the Methodist Church, after much prayer, assigned Reverend Wirick to a permanent church. Having visited Monticello many times while traveling on his circuit, and being well acquainted with many of its most prominent citizens—as well as, most importantly, with a Methodist church already established—this calling from above was quickly followed. Settling into Monticello went well for the Wiricks: land was purchased, and in 1831 the reverend had a large, elegant, colonial-style two-story home constructed.

The reverend was quite popular, with his powerful voice, handsome physique, intelligent mind and eloquence in preaching. With his entertaining conversation and his and Adeline's unfailing hospitality, they were soon the talk of the town. Always the hub of social gatherings, their home was often overflowing with guests pouring out of the home and onto the large porches. The days turned into years, and these would be the happiest times of their lives. The socials and bountiful suppers continued.

The Wiricks hosted an elaborate New Year's Eve party on December 31, 1860. The unseasonably warm weather as midnight approached found the ladies on the veranda sipping mint juleps and discussing the latest town gossip. The men were in the parlor, and the smell of sweet-flavored tobacco wafted into the hall, leaving a pleasant odor lingering throughout.

The men were debating important matters: the talk of an impending war for states' rights. This war would pit the Northern and Southern states against one another, as well as, at times, brother against brother. The men had varying opinions but all shared one: if the war did come, it would be over after one battle.

The following April, four short months later, with the firing on Fort Sumter, the war began. That same month, Florida's governor Madison S. Perry called for a regiment of infantry to serve at Pensacola. A volunteer company was at once formed in Jefferson County and mustered into the Confederation service with the belief that the boys and men would return home soon; they honorably and excitedly marched off to war, a war that wasn't to end until four years later.

During the trying days of the war, the Wiricks made every attempt to maintain a normalcy in their household. Holding to their status, they continued to host social gatherings, fix hot meals for the injured soldiers convalescing from their injuries in private homes in Monticello and pray for the widows.

During the weekly prayer meetings, the reverend and his flock always included a prayer for peace and for their way of life to soon return. The war finally ended on April 18, 1865; however, their way of life would never again be the same.

It would hold many promises and many tragic disappointments. It was the beginning of a long, painful struggle, far longer and more difficult than anyone could have realized. It was the beginning of a struggle that is not yet finished, with its everlasting memories forever imprinted on Monticello.

Soon thereafter, Jefferson County's brave and defeated boys in gray returned home, many with the lingering effects of untreated injuries; awaiting them were a devastated economy and landscape.

When the Wiricks and the other citizens of Jefferson County and Monticello thought that things could not get worse, the Reconstruction period began, in an attempt to reunite the country. With Reconstruction came the scalawags, whom many called turncoats. Reverend Wirick called these native white Southerners who supported Reconstruction Judases. The scalawags were soon followed by the carpetbaggers, unscrupulous Northerners arriving in town toting tapestry bags used to carry their possessions. What homes, land and farms the Yankees had not already burned or pilfered, these men tried to buy for pennies on the dollar.

Reverend Wirick became one of their victims. Refusing to sell, he was forced to remove himself and his family from his Monticello home. His dear, sweet, charming Adeline pined for her Monticello home for the rest of her days on earth.

By 1871, the home had seen its third ownership since the Wiricks: the Thomas Simmons family. These new and last owners hailed from South Carolina, the birth state and home state of Reverend Wirick—the new mistress of the house would even be called Adeline.

Thomas and Adeline Simmons and their large brood of offspring established themselves in Monticello, and like the Wiricks they, too, enjoyed socializing. Once again the home was filled with gaiety and laughter. Their children soon reached adulthood, married and started families of their own—that is, the majority of the brood. Their daughter, Katherine, was destined to remind single. Affectionately known as Miss Katie, she had a love of music and often taught music lessons to the town's children. Miss Katie was also business-minded and independent woman and freethinker. She owned and operated a coffin shop in the rear of Monticello Drug Company, situated conveniently next door. Much of her business came from owners of the many plantations north of town. When the angel of death would come calling for a family member or servant, plantation owners would have their help hitch up a buckboard and ride into town. They would purchase a coffin from Miss Katie and return to the plantation for the burial on their land's cemetery.

In 1935, at the age of 98, when asked for her occupation by the traveling census taker, she wrote "undertaker" on his form without hesitation. As her 100th year of life was approaching, she laid her head down one night and had dreams of an earlier time, when the house was filled with guests and the music from the old piano could be heard throughout the neighborhood. She thought about how she would remain forever in this place, so full of memories, and she peacefully passed on into her life's next journey.

The home stayed in her family for many more years. In 1964, the Jefferson County Historical Society acquired the home from her great-niece to preserve a piece of Jefferson County history. The home is listed on the National Register of Historic Places.

Through the years, townsfolk or tourists passing through—stopping by Monticello's post office directly across the street from the house—from time to time have happened to look over and see a lady in a pink dress standing at the home's attic window. Startled and fearful that somehow the lady had gotten herself locked into the stately house, they have called the police, alerting them as to what they saw.

It is not uncommon for the lady to make an appearance for tour goers who attend the historic Monticello ghost tour. The "pink lady" stills appears to enjoy having company. Tour goers occasionally have the opportunity to see one of the old rocking chairs on the porch begin rocking as they arrive at the house.

The lady in pink's true identify is unknown, whether she is gracious Adeline Wirick returning to the place she so loved and was made to abandon or Miss Katie staying on in the house she vowed to never leave. For those who have seen her, the memory of the lady in pink will forever be etched into the recesses of their minds.

THE MYSTERIOUS STREET

Centuries before Monticello's stately homes and historical old buildings were built, the land was inhabited by Native Americans referred to as the culture of Weedon Island. They planned a hierarchical society and constructed massive earthwork mounds as expressions of their religious beliefs. Letchworth Mounds, an archaeological site forty-six feet high just a few miles west of Monticello proper, is the state's tallest prehistoric ceremonial mound, with artifacts and evidence of nearly ten thousand years of human habitation found at this site. It is believed that sacred sites such as these mounds are linked together by mysterious alignments on the landscape. These ancient sites can be situated in a straight line ranging from one or two to several miles in length. Powerful, invisible earth energies are said to connect various sacred sites—such as churches, temples, stone circles, burial sites and other locations of spiritual importance—and these locations appear to have altered the form of the earth's magnetic field. These energies push and pull against each other just like magnets.

Incidents of ongoing paranormal activity are a common occurrence in areas surrounding these sites. Scientific evidence has proven that electromagnetic fields can affect the body and mind. The effects of this type of energy are said to include feelings of "tingling" on the skin and the hairs standing on end. Even though the energy cannot be heard, it is thought to produce vibrations on a frequency too low for the human ear and provoke feelings of dizziness and unbalance; on occasion, if the energy is strong enough, it is thought to be able to cause feelings of nausea and headaches. These symptoms mirror those often described by people who feel the presence of a ghostly spirit.

Documented paranormal evidence suggests that one out of every three homes or businesses in Monticello is presently haunted or has in the past experienced a haunting. Sedona, Arizona, and Cassadago, Florida, are just two of the many other locations in North American that have these same "energy fields." They, like Monticello, experience an abundance of ghostly encounters.

In the early days of Monticello, family homesteads were situated very near Letchworth Mounds. Stories of ghosts and objects levitating can be found in old family journals handed down through the generations. The "spirits" were so bad in one homesteader's cabin that the man of the house, being of Norwegian descent, built a "spirit trap" consisting of webs or nets of threads woven over hoops or other framework that were placed on paths leading to and from the mounds and at the entrance to his cabin. The principle behind this was that while straight lines facilitated the passage of spirits, convoluted or tangled lines of threads or cord could ensnare them and hinder their movements.

Parapsychologists have found that most poltergeist cases have occurred in areas of these powerful "magnetic earth energies." The mysterious earth energies create a weather anomaly on Dogwood Street: whether it is the heat of August or the cold of January, this street always has a temperature at ten degrees cooler than on any other street in town. An additional anomaly experienced by those who frequent Dogwood Street during evening strolls is the presence of cool breezes. While strolling down the street, a breeze will blow past you, causing the hair on the back of your neck to rise. The only problem is that when you look at any foliage on the side of the street, the leaves are still and silent.

The darkness together with the earth's energies has created spine-tingling encounters for those folks who find themselves walking down this street. On a recent unseasonably warm October night, a young honeymooning couple visiting and lodging in Monticello found themselves on Dogwood Street when the darkness of the fall night came quickly. This particular night, an unexpected fog rolled in, even though the temperature was a warm and balmy seventy-eight degrees. The couple begin shivering, as a bone-chilling wind seemingly engulfed them. They continued walking east with a feeling of impending doom looming over their every step. They huddled a little closer and held hands a little tighter, and then, in the dense fog, they could barely make anything out when they suddenly saw two persons walking west toward them.

It did not take long before the realization of the situation hit them. Although the two figures in the darkness and fog continued coming toward them, they never seemed to get nearer. When the couple reached the intersection with Mulberry Street, they stopped momentarily under the streetlamp and embraced. As they turned to continue their walk under the illumination of the streetlamp, to their disbelief the two figures had stopped right in front of them. Trying to reason with themselves as to why they could see right through these two figures, and reluctant to believe, "fight or flight" took over, and they decided to start running. To their astonishment, the figures took one step forward, walking right through them. Scared, shaken and stupefied, with legs feeling like they were anchored to the pavement, they eventually were able to recompose themselves and make their way back to their lodging, exhausted and confused. They sat up talking the rest of the night, trying to make some sense of the night's frightening events. In finality, they concurred that they had genuinely had a "haunted honeymoon."

With the earth's veins of energy running through it, just like the veins in one's arms, compounded by the additional earth energies deriving from the sacred mounds and ghosts' needing of energy to exist, it is believed that they are drawn to this road like a magnet and come and go at will.

Once ghosts are "energized," they then have the ability to manifest as apparitions; some appear as a smoky form of the living, and some can look amazingly like the entity did during its earthly existence. These apparitions often will interact with the living and return to a place that is familiar to them. They often have a purpose and will attach to a favorite object; sometimes they will attempt to make right a wrong done to them or a wrong they had done to someone else.

THE BRAVE SHERIFF AND THE OLD JAIL

The old jail in Monticello was contracted to be built in 1846 by John Stevens. It was set to be built between present Pearl Street and High Street. Waukeenah and Cherry would be to the east and west. The building was to be thirty-four feet wide and forty feet long. The walls were to be built of brick two feet thick. The ceiling partitions and walls would be built out of lumber and nailed together with wrought-iron nails. The iron cages put on the upper floor were to be ten feet squared and seven feet tall. The total cost of building the Monticello jail was about $3,000.

Things could get pretty rough in the late 1800s in Jefferson County. Courthouse records show common offenses in Monticello included assault and battery, cattle theft, forgery, gambling, false imprisonment, debt, libel, enticing slaves, stealing slaves, selling spirituous liquors to slaves, malicious mischief and brawling. Many of these crimes were punished by fines ranging anywhere between six and a half cents to a dollar. More severe crimes, such as larceny, were punished by stripes being laid on the bare back of the offender. Crimes such as murder were punishable by hanging, but convictions on homicides were rare, as the accused person usually fled into the unexplored wilderness or went into hiding out of the area.

Thompson Brooks Simkins, or T.B. as he was affectionately known, was sheriff in Monticello from 1881 to 1883 and from 1889 to 1899. Law

The sounds of moans and slamming cell doors have been heard coming from the old jail. Built in 1848 as Jefferson County's first jail, the bricks were all molded and kilned on a local plantation by slave labor.

enforcement was in the Simkins family blood; his father, Smith Simkins, was the first sheriff of Jefferson County. Thompson was a very prestigious and wealthy member of the community. On top of his thirteen years of civil service as sheriff, he was also a financial backer for the railroad, was the contractor who completed the new Jefferson Hotel, owned a livery stable in town and was also president of Monticello's trade board. He was also a farmer, harvesting thirteen barrels of Irish potatoes on a half-acre jail lot in town. Sadly, in 1889, Mr. Simkins's lovely home was destroyed in a fire. He immediately started work on a new home, which was finished within the same year. Simkins also loved to raise livestock and was said to have had the finest pair of mules ever seen in Florida. In 1877, his pair of horses took "best pair of matched horses" at the Thomasville, Georgia Fair. He also raised pureblooded dogs and once sold his own personal setter for $120.

Sheriff Simkins was a bit of a legend in Florida. He started his career with some great detective work that led to the solving of a string of serial burglaries that had plagued the town in 1889. He patiently staked out a location night after night until finally he caught the burglar, who turned out to be a city policeman. He received widespread notoriety for his capture of one of the gangs from the area. In 1889, he caught the outlaw Rivers Love—his notorious gang had wrecked havoc on Florida for years. Love later escaped from prison and burglarized a business in Monticello, but within a few short hours, Sheriff T.B. Simkins had him back in the jail. Love then escaped from prison again and returned to Monticello. This time, Rivers Love added murder to his list of crimes in Monticello, when he robbed and then murdered a man in town. The sheriff again caught him and returned him to prison. Four other members of the gang were also put behind bars, and Simkins was hailed as a hero for busting up one of the worst gangs in the country.

On December 29, 1899, Sheriff Thompson Brooks Simkins was shot in the line of duty. The sheriff was trying to arrest fugitive Will Gorman, a black man who had shot at the sheriff of Leon County and was also wanted for several murders. Simkins and his men closed in on the home where Gorman was hiding. T.B. kicked the door in, and then two shots were fired from a Colt .44, piercing his chest and killing him. Will Gorman then fled the house, followed by the sheriff's posse, who shot him down as he tried to flee the scene. News of the good sheriff's death traveled far and wide, and newspapers all over the state reported the terrible tragedy. It was said that there was hardly a man in the state who was as well known or beloved as Simkins.

Thompson Brooks Simkins was survived by his wife and five children. He was laid to rest in Roseland Cemetery, and in 1912, when his wife, Sallie, died, a monument was erected for Sherriff Simkins on their family plot. It reads: "He laid down his life while doing his duty, and was as much a martyr in the public service as if he had died amidst the smoke of battle." His monument can easily be found, as it is the tallest on the grounds. The apparition of an old woman in a lovely long green dress has been seen over the years at the Simkins plot. Visitors to Roseland will sometimes hear the sound of a woman sobbing and will turn to see the figure in her green dress, kneeling down by the monument. If she is approached, she fades away before people can get close to her. In close inspections, sometimes what look like teardrops can be seen on T.B. Simkins's gravestone.

In May 1997, Simkins was remembered for his valiant service and death in the line of duty and was added to the National Law Enforcement Memorial.

While Sheriff T.B. Simkins's body may lie in Roseland, it is said that he haunts the old jail in Monticello. It should be no surprise to us, since so much of his time was spent minding prisoners and keeping up with his other duties around the jail. Many have heard the clanging of cell doors coming from the old abandoned building, and sometimes even the jingling of the old sheriff's keys can be heard as he makes his late-night rounds. Sightings of a man in an old-fashioned suit with a gun on his hip, wandering the grounds, have been reported by some of the police officers who used to work in the adjacent building. So if you are exploring around the jail on a dark night and happen to come across a stately looking gentleman with dark hair and sharp features, just tip your hat and bid him a good night; you can rest assured that T.B. Simkins is just running his rounds in Monticello, making sure that all is well.

THE DUELING OAK

Although dueling was outlawed and considered a misdemeanor after 1829, dueling was so ingrained in the customs of Jefferson County citizens that it was the common resort of people who felt that their honor had been besmirched.

The objective of a duel was not necessarily to kill or even wound the opponent. Duels were all about honor and bravery. The chance of dying in a pistol duel was relatively slim. The old guns, with the flintlock mechanism, often misfired. And even in the hands of an experienced shooter, accuracy was not always possible. Pistols had to be discharged within three seconds; to take aim for a longer time was considered dishonorable.

In America, duels were fought by men from all walks of life. Many of America's most important citizens defended their honor on dueling grounds. One of the most remembered duels took place on July 11, 1804, between Alexander Hamilton and Aaron Burr. The end of their longstanding political and personal battle was to be settled once and for all. The duel was held over in a New Jersey field. Hamilton was mortally wounded, and Burr would be found wanted for murder.

Up until 1865, when the Civil War ended, there was a dispute between Florida and Georgia over the boundary on the north side of Jefferson

County. As a kind of no-man's land, the area became a dueling site for the northern part of Florida.

A gigantic oak planted more than two hundred years ago, simply referred to as the "Dueling Oak," still stands today in all of its majestic glory, with its limbs reaching high toward the heavens.

Locally known as the Old Cotton Trail, motorists can still today travel down this ancient old road with its ruddy blacktop that suddenly turns to red clay. Once you proceed forward on the red clay road, you get an eerie feeling of stepping back in time, and if you listen carefully, you can hear the sounds of horse-drawn wagons making their way to town with a load of cotton. The road, with its canopy oaks, gives off the effect of dusk even for the midday traveler.

Even the novice driver cannot reach the end of the road without seeing the Dueling Oak. As if to claim its place in Jefferson County history, it proudly stands in the center of the road.

During the active dueling years, many men would defend their honors at this location, none better known than the duel between Leigh Read and Augustus Alston that took place on December 12, 1839. Augustus Alston, a veteran of the Seminole Wars, was one of the movers and shakers of Florida politics. Leigh Read was a veteran as well, with opposing political views. Both men had been having a longstanding verbal feud. Read turned down the challenge for the offer of a duel with another political rival, stating that if he was going to duel, it would only be with Augustus Alston. At the urging of friends, Alston accepted, challenging him in return. The weapons of choice were rifles. The terms of the duel were decided on: it would be "duel until dead." Betting started among other political figures as to who would be left standing, with the majority betting that Alston would be the winner. Read, knowing that he was up against a sharpshooting expert, was considered a doomed man.

On the appointed day of the duel, the two met as dawn was breaking, with a chill in the wintery air and the morning dew on the ground. Read arrived with his coffin and burial shroud. The confident Alston instructed his sisters to prepare a "victory banquet" for himself and his friends upon his return. Alston's wife accompanied him to the duel.

Carrying out the terms of the duel, at ten paces they were each to turn and fire. Alston, in his haste, fired his weapon before he aimed it. Read aimed and fired, hitting Alston in the chest. As he lay bleeding to death, his wife vowed that she would have the bullet that killed him do the same to Leigh Read. Alston's sisters, upon hearing news of the death of their brother, ordered that the bullet to be removed from his chest and had it recast. Once this was accomplished, they talked their surviving brother, Willis, into returning from his home in Texas and killing Read with the same bullet that killed Augustus.

A month later, Read was celebrating at an old hotel in nearby Tallahassee. The festive occasion marked the opening of the Florida legislature, and he had been elected speaker of the house. To his shocked surprise, Willis Alston entered the ballroom and attempted to kill him—unsuccessfully.

Willis fled from the area after this, for a time staying with distant family in Texas, Although the incident was not forgotten, Read did let his guard down. In the spring of 1841, walking with a friend down what is now Monroe Street in Tallahassee, unbeknown to most everyone Willis had returned. As Read took his morning walk, Willis emerged from the bushes and came up behind him, shooting him in the back with a rifle. Fulfilling his sisters' wishes, he used the same bullet that had killed his brother. With Read's eyes focused on him, Willis put a fatal shot in his head.

Willis was arrested but managed to escape from jail. Some months afterward, a doctor who had been a friend of Read's was living in the state of Texas and came upon a man who looked familiar, recognizing him to be Willis Alston. Later, as he approached Willis on horseback, a confrontation ensued in which Willis shot and killed the doctor.

Once again, he was thrown into jail for committing a murder. Before he could be taken before a jury and tried, a lynch mob broke him out of jail. This was the last anyone was to ever see of Willis, but seeing Augustus again has become highly probable.

Another well-known and frequent dueler was one of Monticello's most famous residents. Monticello was one the last places you probably would expect to find a member of the Bonaparte family, Charles Louis Napoleon "Achilles" Murat, along with his wife, Catherine Willis Gray. His mother was Caroline Bonaparte, sister of Napoleon Bonaparte, thus making Achilles the nephew of Napoleon. He lived in the area during Florida's territorial and early statehood days. During the early phase of the Seminole Wars, and for the previous three years, he was a lieutenant colonel of Florida's militia.

About 1825, Murat bought the land that he would later call Lipona Plantation east of Tallahassee. The name "Lipona" is an anagram of Napoli (Naples), the kingdom over which Achilles was once destined to rule. Insisting that he be called Prince Murat, he would be known by this for the rest of his life. The prince was known to be rather eccentric and had an aversion to water both for drinking and bathing. His personal hygiene and grooming habits were atrocious. The prince's wife, Catherine, insisted that the servants keep a pot of vanilla simmering on the hearth to mask the odor that announced his presence. Incidentally, the prince lost Lipona due to a gambling debt.

The prince reportedly had his first duel at eighteen years of age in Paris, over debts incurred by his much older and worldly girlfriend at the time, Cory Pearl.

During his years in the Monticello area, the prince would be challenged by Judge David Macomb to a duel in 1834. Beginning with a dispute due to Murat's slaves stealing Macomb's hogs, the bad blood escalated some time later while both were running for political office. At a public forum, Murat called Macomb a liar, and the duel occurred about three days later. During the ensuing gunfight, Macomb shot one of Murat's fingers off. Murat claimed to have put a bullet through Macomb's shirt. Both men, however, survived their injuries and walked away. If you should find yourself on this rural red clay road in the backwoods of Jefferson County in this godforsaken area during a full moon, you may witness what many local folks, including law enforcement, have seen: the distinctive ghostly figures of men dressed in clothing from another time and place, walking down the road away from the old tree.

Another ghostly event is the figures of two men who are seen sitting side by side on one of the massive tree limbs. Once they become aware of being watched, they quickly fade away.

The Big Bend Ghost Trackers team has found itself at the site late at night and can attest to its chilling atmosphere and the overwhelming feeling of dread at approaching it.

ALL ABOARD

Railroad stations have always been prime scenes for hauntings. It's no wonder with all of the hustle and bustle that goes on there that so many emotions forever etched in time. Imagine the heartbroken woman waving goodbye to her lover as she desperately tries to get one last glimpse of him in the window before the train pulls away. Imagine the joy and excitement felt by the little girl on the platform as she eagerly awaits her daddy's train. Imagine the passion felt as long-parted lovers embrace and are reunited.

The first engines were a marvel to behold, and as people stood at the station watching these iron giants roll in, the excitement and wonder was so great that the air became alive and full of energy. Also, the sheer number of people passing through the station alone over all those years makes it ripe for a residual haunting. This seems to be the case with the train depot in Lloyd, here in Jefferson County.

Lloyd was settled by prominent men like General William Bailey and Colonel James Scott. They cleared the land and built family homesteads, and Bailey built a gristmill on the nearby creek's edge. The first station here was called Bailey's Mill, after the general. Later, after the railroad to Tallahassee was completed, the name of the station was changed from Bailey's Mill to Number Two. For a long time, people still referred to

Voices from bygone days can still be heard on the old train platform.

it affectionately as Bailey's Mill, but soon the memory faded. After the Florida Indian Wars, a prominent carpenter named Walter Lloyd came to the area. He settled and opened up a business. He later married Sallie Dry Leonard, who had inherited a rich and fertile plantation passed down to her from her father. Lloyd became a very successful farmer and was so popular among the citizens that when they positioned to have Number Two changed to a more appropriate name, they opted for "Lloyd."

The first railroad project in Florida was started in 1834 and, by 1856, had grown by leaps and bounds thanks to the Internal Improvement Fund. Before this, the main mode of transportation was a stagecoach line running from Jacksonville through Madison and Monticello to Tallahassee. It took about six days to get from Jacksonville to Tallahassee. The first cars on the road were not operated by steam but rather were pulled by stalwart mules driven in tandem. Large amounts of merchandise were transported, mostly cotton—between twenty and thirty thousand bales of cotton annually.

People from all over gathered to gaze in wonder at the first engine as it came over the branch road from Drifton heading to Monticello. When the "Old Bailey" appeared, it was decorated with wreathes, flowers and streamers. It was named after one of its strongest promoters, General William Bailey. The next two decades would find travel by steam an assured fact, and much freight was moved at a quicker pace than it had been in the past. The railroad through Jefferson County was seen as a marvel of speed and efficiency by all who saw it. It was seen as a way to connect and bring the country together. Soon, in 1886, a second railroad was built between Monticello and Thomasville and then connected Thomasville to Savannah. For many years, the directors of Atlantic Coastline contemplated extending the railroad down Florida's west coast, which would correspond with the Florida East Coast Railroad. When finally completed, a direct route from Tampa to Chicago was put in the works.

Another stretch of the Atlantic Coastline railroad was laid through the county to Fanlew, where lumber workers from Jefferson County had made a small settlement. It was used to transport supplies to the large sawmills. It also carried goods from the mills into the surrounding communities.

In 1926, a right-of-way through Jefferson County was surveyed and purchased and was then put into use. This caused the train to pass two miles east of Monticello, where the neat brick station had been erected. At this distance from town, folks found it a significant expense to pay to be transported and have their goods transported all the way to the station. Outrage hit the good people of Monticello when they found that, in secret, the old train track had been completely removed during the night as they slept. Since this happened without their consent or knowledge, a lawsuit was brought into action, but unfortunately no redress was ever obtained. Monticello never truly recovered from this blow.

For more than half a century, trains stopped in Lloyd for dinner as they passed through on their way back and forth to Jacksonville. They would stop at the Whitfield House, where the widow of General Whitfield would play hostess to the weary travelers. Dinner would be a lavish affair, and the tables were loaded down with an abundance of fine southern foods. Servants would pass out both hot and cold drinks as patrons indulged in the many delicacies. Sometimes two trains would bring as many as two hundred people to these grand dinners at the Whitfield House. When the number of people was so great that they could not accommodate them all, the widow's daughter, Ida H. Dennis, would help with the overflow—later she would take up the business for her mother when she was no longer able to handle it due to her old age. Ida successfully ran the business for many years. Later, a dining cart was added to the train when people began to press for faster transit times, cutting twenty minutes from the travel time and, sadly, putting an end to an era of prosperity for the Whitfield House. In short order, it withered up and eventually closed.

Today the old train depot in Lloyd is used as the post office. Workers there have reported many strange occurrences. Most commonly heard in the backroom of the building is the murmur of a crowd, as though the room is full of bustling people. This room was once the waiting room for passengers as they waited for the train to pull into the station. Many an employee has poked his head into the room upon hearing the chatter, only to find it empty and silent. Also, a bell has often been heard ringing in the back of the building, which is the old train depot platform. This is sometimes accompanied by the ghostly voice of the long-passed conductor crying out, "All aboard!" Feel free to visit the old depot in Lloyd and make sure you quietly listen for the sounds of people's feet shuffling on the old platform, as well as the voices from times long since passed that still linger in the air, reminding of us of bygone days when this place was busy and full of life.

HENRY WEST AND HIS LOVELY BRIDE

Henry West was born in January 1863. Like so many of Monticello's residents, he was a farmer. One of the top crops that West grew was watermelons, as they were a significant cash crop in the area. The soil and weather conditions in the area proved to be a great combination for watermelons. During the late 1800s, a typical farm would be about one hundred acres in size. New inventions had helped people to farm more efficiently. In 1838, John Deere invented the steel plow. Reapers made the harvesting of crops much easier, and threshers helped farmers to separate grain or seed from straw. From 1860 to 1890, farmers doubled their production of crops like wheat.

Henry West was seen as quite the eligible bachelor in Monticello, but he had it in mind that marriage wasn't for him. He had managed just fine so far, so why should he tie himself down with a marriage. Yes, he could do just fine all on his own, but this soon changed when the lovely Sarah moved across the way.

Miss Sarah Clark, born in October 1868, was a beautiful young woman of impeccable taste. She, however, had some very liberal and modern notions of what a woman's prerogative was and what was considered appropriate for a lady. Miss Clark was a feminist with ideas far before their time, and those ideas were not always embraced by the majority of the old-fashioned folks in Monticello, Florida. You see, in the 1800s, women were second-class citizens. A woman was expected to restrict her sphere of interest to her home and family. Women were not encouraged to receive a real education or pursue professional careers. Even though grade-school girls often scored notably higher than boys, they were usually not given the chance to pursue forms of higher education. Instead, their continuing education consisted of learning wifely duties such as cooking, sewing, cleaning and preparing for motherhood. After marriage, women didn't have the right to own their own property, retain guardianship of children, keep wages or even sign contracts. Also, all women were denied the right to vote. Interest in politics was not considered a proper topic for a woman to discuss or show interest in. This, however, did not stop young Sarah from getting into lively, opinionated debates.

First it was just a smile shared between the two, and then a comment on the weather or a kind word. Before long, Henry was courting Sarah, and a romance was starting to blossom. He was soon smitten and had eyes only for her. He found himself confessing that he could not imagine his life without her and wanted to spend the rest of his with her. Sarah confessed that she loved him, too, and also could see herself becoming Mrs. Henry West, but her hand was not so easily won. She told Henry that she would only agree to marry him if he put all of his property and assets into her name. This was simply unheard of at the time—not just in Jefferson County but anywhere in Florida.

In the United States, women historically were denied property rights. The women's rights movement in the late 1800s increased civil rights for women in many areas, including their right to own property. Throughout most of the 1800s, a woman's property was under the control of her husband. This was left over from British law, which ordered that a woman's legal rights were suspended and given to her husband while she was married. Early laws in Florida noted that women had to pay property taxes on property but could not even own it.

In the United States, one exception was made in the instance of a prenuptial contract. Most states accepted these contracts, but few couples signed them. Parents of wealthy young ladies would sometimes insist on these contracts to keep family property in a trust for their daughter and her heirs. Widows would sometimes draw up a prenuptial contract before getting remarried to protect their previous assets. Without a prenuptial, the property a woman had before her marriage would be under her husband's control afterward. This meant that a husband could sell his wife's jewelry and heirlooms, spend her wages or squander her inheritance without any ramifications. However, by 1900, every state had given married women some sort of control over their own property.

Henry didn't care if it was unorthodox. He was so in love that he agreed right away, and theirs was believed to be the first prenuptial agreement in the state of Florida. Miss Sarah Clark and Mr. Henry West were married on December 2, 1891. They never had children, but despite that, theirs was a long and happy marriage. Even in their old age, they doted on each other like young lovers. Unfortunately, Henry passed away on September 4, 1920, leaving Sarah a widow. She never remarried, claiming that she would always be Mrs. Henry West. There is no recorded date for the death of Sarah West, but census documents show her alive in 1935, so we know that she lived to see women get the right to vote in 1920.

Both neighbors and passersby of the Henry West House have seen apparitions of an older couple both in the home and on the property. One lady claimed that she saw them both on the porch as clear as day, and another says that she saw a woman in quaint old clothing strolling through the yard with an older, well-dressed man in a suit. She stopped to ask them for directions to a home she was looking for in the area. The woman just shook her head and pointed down the street. The young woman looked in that direction and then looked back, but the old-fashioned couple had vanished. It's really no surprise that the Wests are spending their afterlife together in their beloved home. After all, as in love as they were, a little thing like death isn't going to keep them apart.

LITTLE LULA

L ittle Lula Emery was a beautiful and spirited yet shy little girl. The daughter of merchant S.C. Emery and his wife, C.T. Emery, Lula loved playing with her dolls, having tea parties and doing all of the other little games that young girls like to play. With her long curls, freckles and sweet, round face, she was the light of her parents' life, and they tried to indulge her with all of the things that make children happy. Lula loved to play with her friends and family, but was always shy when it came to strangers.

She loved nursery rhymes, and playing "Ring Around the Rosie" was her favorite. She and her mother would sing the song, dancing around in a circle, giggling and falling to the ground at the end. While "Ring Around the Rosie" is a beloved song to children, it's actually quite macabre. It was thought to have originated in Europe during the time of the plague, or Black Death. The first line, "Ring around the roses," was thought to represent the rosy red rash on the face that was one of the first symptoms of the plague. The second line, "Pocket full of posies," was a reference to the bouquets of herbs and flowers people would carry in their pockets to give themselves protection and to try to cover up the smell of death all around them. There are two variants of the final line. "Achoo, achoo, we all fall down," was the first version, which was a reference to the coughing and sneezing that marked the final symptom before death. The other version, "Ashes, ashes, we all fall down," referenced the cremation of the bodies and, sometimes, entire homes that were burned down after death. While we are surprised at the morbid nature of children's rhymes like this one, we need to think about the fact that life was a lot harder back then, and death was a major part of life experienced by all at a much younger age. Perhaps songs like this were a way for children to brush up on the very real subject of death.

Little Lula filled the Emery house with laughter and the patter of tiny feet as she pushed her dolls down the hall in their carriage and played hide-and-seek in every room. But soon, laughter would turn to tears, as a new danger came to plague the city of Monticello. Merchants and travelers returning to Monticello were bringing the disease known as yellow fever back with them. Little Lula, who was normally a bundle of energy, was tired and complained to her mother of dizziness, headache and an aching all over her body. Upon inspection, Lula's mother felt her high-grade fever, and a doctor was called in. Her parents' worst fears were confirmed when the doctor told them that she had yellow fever.

Yellow fever had already become an epidemic in Jefferson County. The death count rose and rose, filling the cemeteries and leaving very few families untouched. Lula's parents prayed fervently by her bedside for her recovery as she suffered in her weakened state for three or four days. Then, as if their prayers were answered, she began to get well. The fever vanished, and Lula was running about, playing as if nothing had happened. But unfortunately, this short remission was the telltale sign of this disease. Within days, she was back in bed, her fever higher than ever. Sweet Lula's light freckled skin turned yellow and her tongue bright red, to her parents' horror. She began to bleed from her mouth and nose. She also began to fade in and out of consciousness and was delirious when she was awake. Soon after, on May 25, 1888, Lula Emery passed away, just a little after her third birthday.

Yellow fever was a viral infection transmitted by mosquitoes. The insects became carriers by feeding on an infected person. Yellow fever symptoms started three to six days after exposure. The fever, which typically ranged from 102 to 104 degrees Fahrenheit, came on suddenly. In this first stage, other symptoms included headache, a rose-red face, nausea, vomiting and muscle aches. The gums and nose may have bled, and the person was likely to be restless and cranky. The symptoms typically lasted for two or three days. Then, those who were lucky enough made a recovery. For those who were not, however, there was a brief remission in which the patient's symptoms would disappear for several days. Then, fever and other symptoms returned. Jaundice, a yellowing of the skin and eyes that gives the disease its name, occurred, indicating the failing liver. The tongue would then turn a bright red color, and bleeding from the nose, mouth and intestinal tract would begin. In some cases, the person would vomit black blood and become confused and delirious until falling into a coma.

Yellow fever became a devastating plague to Jefferson County. During the 1888 yellow fever epidemic, the government tried to help by offering railroad transportation out of the area. William F. Hawley described the panicked scene at a crowded railroad station: "The trains were packed to the limit, even the roofs of the cars were crowded with terrified citizens… Some people in their haste left their homes with fires burning, food in preparation for the noonday meal, and doors wide open." Many remedies were tried, such as burning barrels of tar in the street to disinfect the air or by spraying a mixture of coppers, sulfur and lime in the homes of the infected. It wasn't until later in the year 1900 when U.S. Army physician James Carroll, with the help of pathologist Walter Reed, proved that yellow fever was contracted from the bite of an infected mosquito. He allowed an infected mosquito to bite him and developed a severe case of the disease.

Little Lula's death was quite hard on her parents, who buried their beloved little angel at what is known today as the 1827 Cemetery. They had a lovely, ornate headstone made for her, with a little lamb on it, which was the last thing they could think to do for their daughter in death. Knowing their little girl's fear of strangers, they bought up the surrounding plots around her grave so that no one would be buried near her. Visitors to the cemetery have reported many encounters with young Lula. Maternal women have, many times, felt small tugs at their clothing when visiting the young girl's grave. People who have been encouraged to play "Ring Around the Rosie" at the grave site have experienced her touch or even heard what sounded like a little girl's laugh. Toys are sometimes left on her grave by kind passersby. Historic Monticello ghost tour participants

Little Lula died of yellow fever at age three, and her parents had her buried at Roseland, where her sweet little spirit can be found.

once witnessed a ball near her grave being pushed back and forth on a windless day. Interesting EVPs (electronic voice phenomena) have also been recorded on audio and video tapes from around her grave.

This all begs the question that many ask about the ghosts of children: why is Lula here, and why didn't she move on? The truth is that no one knows for sure. Perhaps she stayed on to comfort her grieving family, or simply to be with them, and then never moved on, even after they were gone. Whatever the reason for her staying earthbound, all of the evidence seems to indicate that, just as in life, Little Lula seems to be a happy spirit.

THE SPIRITS OF ROSELAND

Roseland Cemetery was established in the heart of Monticello in about 1827. The cemetery is located on Madison Street, three blocks east of Jefferson Street. Lots at Roseland are twenty-four feet square. All of the lots have been sold, so I am afraid that there is not room for one more. Spring and summer find Roseland alive and in bloom with azaleas, roses and countless other sweet-smelling flowers. On moonlit nights, a gentle breeze blows through, giving a reprieve from the heat of day.

The stonemasonry here at Roseland is both beautiful and enduring. There is brickwork that looks the same now as the day it was laid, unique Gothic-style coffin-shaped gravestones and myriad obelisks that can be seen stretching up toward the heavens. Most big cemeteries in the 1840s and 1850s have at least a few of these towering monuments of this pervasive revival style. These Egyptian-influenced works of art were also common among Freemasons of the day.

Many of the prominent figures from the stories in this book are buried at the cemetery. The earthly remains of the Majewskis; Mr. Perkins and his lovely wife, India; the endearing Wests; John Denham and his family; Katie Simmons; Little Lula; and heroes like "Boots" Thomas and Sheriff Simkins are all here at beautiful Roseland. Here are the stories of some of the ghostly encounters and tales from the cemetery.

Many of the historical figures from the stories in this book are buried at Roseland Cemetery.

MR. GRAY SUIT

Samuel Pasco was born in London, England, in 1834 but moved to the United States when he was just a boy. He attended Harvard University before settling in Monticello in 1859. He then took up the post of principal at Waukeenah Academy. When the Civil War began, he enlisted in the army of the Confederate States of America, despite having been in the South just two short years. He fought as a member of the Florida Third Volunteers. He was wounded in battle and captured early on and spent the length of the war imprisoned. When the war ended, he was released, returning to Monticello and resuming his position as principal. He later resigned and became an outstanding lawyer. In 1885, he was president of a convention that created a new constitution for Florida. He served as Speaker in 1887 and was also elected to the U.S. Senate that same year. He was a member of a committee called the Isthmian Canal Commission, which had decided to build a canal in Panama. He later retired and returned to his beloved Monticello, where he died on March 13, 1917. Pasco County, Florida, is named after him.

The ghost known as Mr. Gray Suit is thought to be Samuel Pasco. Always well dressed and refined, just as Pasco always was, Mr. Gray Suit can be caught slinking around various parts of Roseland. Once, during a private cemetery tour with Monticello Ghost Tours, the small group was startled when the apparition of a stately man in a dark-gray suit with a top hat was seen casually leaning against a large tombstone. After this, a gentleman approached the spot where the ghostly figure had been seen, taunting him. He dared him to make his presence known. The man then began to scream and fled the cemetery. As the group gathered under a streetlight to reorganize, he revealed three dark scratches on his arm that he claimed came from Mr. Gray Suit. So if you happen to be exploring Roseland, do remember your manners, because Mr. Pasco was and is a stickler for respect and decorum.

MRS. CARROLE AND THE GREEN-EYED MONSTER

When approaching the Carrole family plot, you will see that Mr. and Mrs. Carrole are buried side by side. However, there is quite a few years' difference between their death dates. Mrs. Carrole was infected with the green-eyed monster of jealousy. She watched her husband at all times and scrutinized his every move. No one knows what it was that made her this way, but people who knew the couple said that it definitely was not her husband's fault. He was kind, generous and loyal to a fault.

Now, there was a young widow in town who supported herself and young children by delivering fresh baked bread and eggs to people's homes. One day, the widow arrived, and Mrs. Carrole was not yet back from her trip into town, where she was attending a meeting of the Ladies Temperance Society. Mr. Carrole kindly invited the young woman into the kitchen, where the two made polite conversation. Mrs. Carrole walked in only to see them smiling and laughing over the widow's breadbasket. Flying into a fit of jealous rage, she picked up her meat cleaver from the counter and began to chase them both. Her husband pleaded their innocence as they ran around and around the kitchen.

The widow, being young and spry, abandoned her basket and ran out the door, fearing to even look back. Poor Mr. Carrole was not so lucky.

He ran through the open doorway with his wife hot on his heels. In his haste, he slipped and fell off the porch, breaking his neck. His wife never truly showed remorse for her actions, always claiming that she was in the right and that he and the lovely widow had been up to no good. On very still days at Roseland, sometimes an unexplained whirlwind will kick up over the Carrole graves. The groundskeepers have seen this so many times that they simply say that the Carroles must be at it again. Even in death poor Mr. Carrole cannot find escape.

THE POPPING STONE

Miss Frances Clover, known as Fannie, was seen by the people of Monticello as a busybody. She was the type to eavesdrop on your conversation and then drop tidbits of your private business all over town. She spied on her neighbors, keeping close tabs on their ins and outs and always adding her two cents about impropriety. At church, she would endlessly gossip abut who wasn't tithing like they should or who had drank a little too much the night before. Fannie's meddling ways did not make her popular with the townsfolk, and when she became sick and passed away long before her time, the turnout at her funeral was very small.

The day after her funeral, the preacher and his wife came to visit Fannie's grave to see if the stone the church had purchased had been installed. They were quite shocked to find the brand-new stone laying

Old stones have been known to unearth themselves and fall forward from time to time.

facedown on the grave. Thinking that some young vandals had disturbed Miss Clover's grave, they immediately went to the groundskeeper, who came out and replanted the stone. He promised to be extra vigilant and keep an eye out to make sure that no one disturbed the grave again. The next morning, he returned early to find that the stone had popped out of the ground again. He fixed the stone, but every morning thereafter the stone would be popped out of the earth and lying facedown on Fannie's grave. There was never any sign of anyone entering the graveyard to possibly disturb it. Over time, the frequency of the stone popping diminished, but it happened for years before a solution was found. Eventually, a concrete base was made to hold the stone in place. This seems to have kept Miss Clover in her place. No one knows for sure why the stone popped up all those years. Perhaps Fannie was angered by the fact that hardly anyone had attended her funeral and paid their respects, and this was her way of making herself heard even in death.

HASTY BURIAL

When you first enter Roseland, you will see some graves with piles of bricks in disorganized heaps. It's quite a contrast from the immaculate brick vaults in the older 1827 section. These are graves from the yellow fever epidemic. With the epidemic came fear and panic; people thought

Victims of yellow fever were sometimes given a hasty burial out of fear that they were still contagious.

that the bodies were contagious, and some in their haste buried the bodies in shallow graves with bricks piled on top of the surface. The graves are unmarked, and the contents of most are now unknown. It's thought that some of these souls are not at rest due to their hasty, improper burial.

THE GHOSTLY LIGHT

The young and beautiful Louisa was married to a man ten years her senior, but theirs was a happy marriage. Louisa's husband was extremely loving and attentive. Sweet Louisa was deathly afraid of the dark, so her husband would make candles for her. Every night, before the sun would go down, he would light her a few candles, and even as she slept, a candle would be burning on her bedside table. Sadly, though, after only a few short years of marital bliss, lovely Louisa died in childbirth. Her poor husband was devastated by the loss of his wife and child. He never

A ghostly light is often seen in the cemetery at night hovering over the grave of young Louisa.

forgot his beloved bride, and every night he could be seen carrying a lit candle to her grave to burn throughout the night. He returned every night until he himself passed on to be reunited with Louisa. Glimpses of a ghostly shining light are sometimes seen hovering throughout the old 1827 section of Roseland, and it's believed that even in death Louisa's dearly beloved returns to illuminate the darkness for her.

THE FIRE

Sometime in the early to mid-1800s, there was a children's home in Jefferson County that caught fire and burned to the ground. On a cold, dark night, while all of the children were sleeping, a spark from the fireplace was said to have caught the wooden floor on fire. The old house, being the tinderbox that it was, went up in flames in the blink of an eye. There were no known survivors. All of the children and the ladies of the house were buried in a mass grave in the old 1827 section of Roseland. There is no marker; the grave can be distinguished from the others by looking for the two large, square brick wall enclosures connected to each other. An abundance of paranormal activity is reported by the grave site. Groundskeepers often hear the sound of laughter during the day. At first, they thought that they were hearing voices of children who were playing hooky from school and were hiding out in the cemetery. Every time they looked, however, no one was ever there. From time to time, toys are left on the grave, and these toys are never in the same place in the morning.

THE BLUE AND THE GRAY

During the Civil War, makeshift hospitals were set up in homes in Monticello. Many times, Yankee boys would be treated right alongside southern boys. Sadly, when many of these brave young men died, no one knew their names, and they were buried in unmarked graves. At Roseland, there is such a place in the 1827 section of the cemetery. A fence encloses about twenty graves, marked only as containing those who served in the Civil War. Here the blue and the gray are buried together,

Gravestones from the Civil War soldiers of both North and South.

with nothing to differentiate between the two. Groundskeepers claim that a ruckus and whirlwind can sometimes be seen inside the fence, as though they are bickering. Quite often, on historic Monticello cemetery tours, the gate to the fence will open all on its own. Once, the Big Bend Ghost Trackers team put American flags on each grave. Upon returning a short time later, they discovered, to their dismay, that nine of the flags were pulled up and sitting in a pile by the open gate. Is it possible that those proud southern boys didn't approve of these Yankee flags?

THE MAD DOCTOR

Henry Grattan Wirt was a simple doctor in Jefferson County. His practice was laidback and quaint before the yellow fever epidemic ravaged Jefferson County. All at once, though, his life was thrown into utter turmoil. Large homes and churches were turned into makeshift hospitals that quickly filled with deathly sick people. The good doctor found himself working for days at a time with barely a wink of sleep. One day, after working himself to the point of sheer exhaustion trying to care for and save as many as he could, he felt as if he could not go on. So he found a quiet place in the back corner of a dark upstairs room, lay down and went to sleep.

While he slept, some others decided to move the bodies that were piling up into the backroom. When they entered and saw the sleeping doctor, they assumed that he was just another dead man and began piling bodies around him and, eventually, over top of him. The doctor was so completely exhausted that he managed to sleep through the whole thing. When he finally awoke, he found himself buried under a mound of dead and festering bodies, unable to even move. This combined his two greatest fears: small spaces and being buried alive. He began to scream and shout and thrash about, desperately trying to free himself from the mountain of human flesh under which he had become trapped. His muffled cries could not be heard downstairs, and his attempts to free himself were in vane. He was trapped there all night.

When morning finally came, and men arrived to bury their dead, they heard strange, beastly sounds emanating from the room. The sounds were described as being similar to a mad dog's growl. They finally dug the doctor out, but by then he appeared to have lost his mind. He refused to speak, making only grunting and growling noises. He never recovered his wits after that. He no longer practiced medicine and rarely left his home. He took to pulling out his own hair and babbling endlessly. Eventually, he was locked up in an insane asylum, where he took his own life.

Doctor Henry Grattan Wirt's grave can be found in the old 1827 section of Roseland. Groundskeepers claim to have heard strange animal noises coming from the vault where he is buried, and several growling sounds reminding one of a rabid animal have been recorded on audio tape.

THE WEEPING WIDOW

A large obelisk adorns the Simkins family plot where Sheriff Simkins and his family are buried. Visitors to Roseland have caught glimpses of a mysterious woman in green. Most were startled by the sounds of a woman's mournful weeping. They turn to see this woman in her green, flowing dress kneeling down and weeping at a grave. Could this be the widow of Sheriff Simkins, still mourning the loss of her fallen husband? Upon approaching the woman, she always fades away, but some claim to have seen the wet droplets from her fresh tears on the good sheriff's gravestone.

ROSELAND'S BABIES

As you explore Roseland, one thing becomes clear very quickly: there are a lot of infant graves. Infant mortality was very high in the 1800s. You were hard-pressed to find a family who didn't lose at least one child. With the yellow fever and the influenza epidemics, Monticello lost more than its fair share of children. Rows of up to six to seven infants and children can be seen in some family plots. The loss to these families must have been devastating. People sometimes hear the cry of a baby near the entrance to Roseland. One woman drove by and heard a baby's cry, so

Between the yellow fever and influenza epidemics in Jefferson County, almost every family felt the loss of a child.

she stopped the car, rushing in toward the sound, thinking that someone had abandoned their baby on this dark and cold night. No child was found, but there are still reports of crying from time to time.

BURIED ALIVE

With progress coming to Monticello, more roads were needed to make travel practical. As a result, roads were put through several city cemeteries. While moving the bodies, some of the coffins were opened. To the utter horror of the men relocating them, they found that some had claw marks inside and that other bodies were flipped upside down. More than a few people had been buried alive. This did not sit well with the good people of Monticello, so they came up with a familiar plan to ensure that this didn't happen to their loved ones in the future. During burial, a string was tied around the person's wrist and run up through the ground and attached to a bell. Then, a family member would sit up all night in the cemetery. This was known as taking "the graveyard shift." They would wait just in case the person, by some small chance, woke up and started to move around, causing the bell to ring. If the bell rang, the person keeping watch was said to have a "dead ringer." They would call for the men folk, and they would come and in great haste dig up the poor soul who had been "saved by the bell."

THE JILTED BRIDE

In the fall of 1920, in what at the time was known as the Dill community (an area today that encompasses the Boston Highway and Florida Highway 19 North in Monticello), the Deloren family had cause to celebrate—even with the fall harvest upon them and many of their kinfolk and neighbors sick with the influenza epidemic that was sweeping the nation like a plague. Pricilla, the family's oldest and only unmarried daughter, had become engaged. Young women in the early 1900s were often pressured into marriage by their families for monetary gain or for stability and status.

Pricilla, nearing the age of twenty-eight, had become the subject of much gossip. With her free-spirited personality, she had been known to smoke a pipe on occasion and take a "swig" from her papa's brown jug. Above all else, Pricilla loved horses and could often been seen riding bareback through the countryside. Many of the country folks said that she could "ride like the wind" and "charm a wild steed."

Through the years, Pricilla's family made many efforts to tame her, but in vain. On Pricilla's eighteenth birthday, her exasperated parents, at the urging of their church pastor, sent Pricilla north to Miss Shaw's Finishing School for Proper Young Ladies in Rhode Island. Unfortunately, this plan backfired, with Pricilla seemingly enjoying the "city" life and picking up a few new bad habits, including hemming her shirt waist dresses to an improper length and wearing dungaree pants.

Pricilla continued to display unladylike behavior during much of the following years, until the month of October in 1919. A nearby farmer had an ailing wife and both of his sons off fighting in World War I. The farmer's recently widowed nephew (an experienced horseman named William, who was referred to as "Wills") arrived from Georgia to help out. Shortly after his arrival, by a chance meeting at a feed and seed store, he and Pricilla met and struck up a conversation regarding horses.

In the following weeks, the family saw what appeared be a miraculous transformation in Pricilla. The dungarees were left behind, and with little persuasion from her mother, Pricilla agreed to accompany her to town to purchase fabric and sewing notions for a new dress.

Pricilla and Wills began courting by year's end with what the families called a whirlwind relationship, and in March 1920, Wills took Pricilla to town to see Rhoda's Royal Circus and the Old Buffalo Wild West Show. On the way home, Wills asked Pricilla for her hand in marriage. Pricilla was ecstatic and immediately said yes. Wills placed an engagement ring on the fourth finger of her left hand.

The belief was that there was a vein running from this finger all the way to the heart. So by wearing a ring on this finger, you are saying that the person who gave you that ring has a direct link to your heart.

Plans were made for a late fall wedding after the fall crops were in and the haying was done. The date was set to be Saturday, November 6, at three o'clock in the afternoon. The bride's and groom's family members and many friends in the community were expected to attend.

Much had to be done to get ready for this joyous occasion. Pricilla and her mother looked through all of the ladies' magazines that were available and decided on a wedding dress design from *Godey's Magazine and Lady's Book*. An appointment was scheduled in early June with Fanny Bush, a seamstress in Tallahassee, and travel arrangements and plans were made. It would be a two-day trip, with mother and daughter renting a room at the Old Leon Hotel, Tallahassee's finest hotel, whose guests mainly consisted of politicians having business at the state capitol.

After arriving at the seamstress's home, many hours were spent looking and fingering fabric samples. A beautiful white satin fabric was chosen with the finest of lace to adorn the long sleeves. Exquisite embroidery and gorgeous hand-sewn beads would be added to make the wedding dress even more stunning. The fabrics and notions would be ordered from New York City and would arrive in four weeks, and it would take another four weeks for the seamstress to complete the dress. A merry widow hat would be ordered from a millinery shop in New Orleans to complete the trousseau.

When the heat from the sultry summer turned to the cool nights of fall, it found Pricilla busying herself with the wedding day preparations. Long evening walks with Wills continued, and the last picnic of the year was planned. Sunday church services and then Sunday dinner afterward, a spread fit for royalty at Pricilla's parents' house, prepared by her mother, was a weekly event.

When October came, Pricilla was enthralled that the last of the wedding plans were in place, after making a decision on the bridal flowers. White roses, white orchids and lilies of the valley were her choice for the bridal bouquet. Her bridesmaids would also carry white, and these flowers (which were customary in that time and place) were often paid for by the groom.

With the hustle and bustle and the arrival of out-of-town family members to help with the wedding, Pricilla failed to take notice of the aloofness that had come over her intended. Wills no longer rushed over to Pricilla's house every evening. He was spending most of his evenings either in his room alone or at the billiards hall.

It was Saturday morning, November 6, and the big day had arrived. All of the ladies in the house were in front of mirrors, primping and fixing hair. Pricilla had chosen the newest hairstyle craze: the pompadour.

Pricilla, with the help of her mother and sisters, readied herself in her wedding attire. Her father had rented a carriage and driver to deliver her to the family's church five miles away. This was the same site her younger sisters had used before her. As the three o'clock hour neared, the wedding guests began arriving. There was no sign of Wills, but Pricilla did not let it concern her, as she believed in the old wives' tale that the bride and groom should not see each other on the day prior to the wedding ceremony. It was thought to cause bad luck.

The pastor welcomed the guests, the organist began to play and the wedding procession came to order and began to make its way down the church aisle. Pricilla, with her head in the clouds, did not notice her groom's absence until she arrived at the altar. Wills's uncle quietly made his way to the church's entrance and, with a wave of his hand, summoned for the pastor. Pricilla's only thoughts were that Wills had met with an accident. Soon, to her sorrow and anguish, she wished she had been correct. It seemed that Wills, while the morning's dew was still on the ground and the sun was still waking up in the East, had quietly packed his belongings, saddled his horse, made his way to the train depot and quickly left town.

Pricilla began to loudly sob and ran from the church. When her family was to next see her, she had managed to somehow make her way back home and taken to her bed. In the days that followed, she became silent and despondent, with her family making every effort to raise her spirits, but to no avail. One month later, her mother—frantic with worry when Pricilla had stopped eating—brought to her room a cup of hot tea and toast and found her firstborn pale and cold. Many say that Pricilla died of a broken heart, while others have said that she took her own life.

The years passed, and many of the townsfolk often talked about Pricilla, the jilted bride. Family members grew old and joined Pricilla on the "other side."

In 2000, a family descendant inherited an old home from a great aunt. The home's attic contained various antiques, including a silk wedding dress found in the bottom of an old trunk. The dress was folded up in an old bed sheet and wrapped in newspaper dated November 8, 1920.

The new homeowner took the silk wedding dress and other antiques to a consignment shop to be sold. The proprietor of the antiques shop thought the dress to be so lovely that she immediately put the dress on an old mannequin and displayed it in the shop's window. As luck would have it, a few weeks later, a mother and her soon-to-be-married daughter just happened to pass by and see the dress. The daughter had a fancy for "old things" and vintage clothing and immediately took a liking to it.

The mother and daughter were both impressed with how new and well cared for the dress looked and agreed to purchase the dress for her daughter if the fit was right. The daughter was then allowed to try on the dress. As she modeled the dress for her mother and the shopkeeper, she felt a twinge of pain in her neck, as if being pricked by a pin. Thinking that the inner facing in the dress's neck perhaps had become stiff with age, she did not give it another thought. The dress would need a few alterations for a better fit, but the price was good and the dress seemed just right. The mother paid for the purchase.

In the car on the way home, the mother and daughter talked and wondered who the bride had been, thinking of various scenarios, all ending in "and they lived happily ever after." As her wedding date neared, the daughter took the dress to be altered. Soon pins were placed here and there on the dress. The seamstress, picking up her scissors to make a small cut to mark the new length, was startled as the young woman let out a horrific groan and appeared to be struggling for breath. Thinking that she was having some sort of asthma attack, the seamstress helped her out of the dress and to a seat.

Bringing the young woman a glass of water and a damp cloth to wipe her red face, the seamstress noticed marks on her neck. The young woman's mother was called and, upon arrival, took note of the marks, which now clearly had taken on the impressions of fingers. After composing herself, the young woman told a story of having had the distinct feeling of being choked, as if someone was pressing their hands around her neck and she could not catch her breath.

Neither the mother nor the daughter had ever had any interest in the supernatural, nor even thought about it. But they came to the fast conclusion that there was something ominous about the dress. They went immediately to the antiques shop where the dress was purchased, showed the marks to the proprietor and asked if the origin of the dress was known. A call was made to the gentleman who had brought the dress to the shop. He reported only that he had found it in a trunk but promised to make some calls to older family members who might be able to shed some light on the identity of the bride. A week later, he arrived at the antiques shop with a grim face and told the story of an old, well-kept family secret. Pricilla was a great-great-cousin of his, and it appeared that she had not "lived happily ever after." On that fateful morning many years before, when her mother found her lifeless body, she had wrapped tightly and knotted around her neck a silk scarf made from a remnant of her wedding dress. The scarf had been diligently hand-sewn by Pricilla to wear on her honeymoon.

Ghosts have been known to attach themselves to an object that held a significance in their lives. Pricilla, in her final moments before death, had only thoughts of her wedding day and her beautiful dress. If Pricilla could not be married in the dress, some way, somehow, from the great beyond, she would make sure that no one else was, either.

Money was returned, and the dress was once again in the possession of the family member. After a few worrisome weeks, out of concern that some other prospective bride in some future day might once again attain the dress, he made the painful decision to burn it.

Reportedly, horrific screams of agony and despair were heard as the dress burned, highlighting again this woman's tortured soul as the last thing she had clung to, the object of her greatest joy and suffering in life, was finally destroyed.

THE HERO

In a just world, Ernest "Boots" Thomas would have returned to his hometown of Monticello after World War II as a celebrated hero. But it was not to be.

"Boots," as he was known, was given the nickname by his father. He was always a brave and handsome young man. Growing up in this small town gave him character. During his high school years, he was a star athlete, participating on most of the school's sports teams. Boots was also an honor roll student. He was popular with the girls, with his dark curly hair and sly smile. After school and on Saturdays, he diligently worked as a bag boy at the local A&P grocery store, always well mannered and respectful to the customers. He was often asked for, especially by the elderly female shoppers.

As his senior year in high school was ending, he contemplated his future. He had always considered a career in the service of his country, but his mother would not hear of it. Then, as if an answer to a mother's prayer, he received a scholarship to study aeronautical engineering at Tri-State College in Angola, Indiana. The following September, in 1941, he left Monticello and made his move to Indiana to attend college. With his spirits high and filled full of hope, he started a new chapter in his life. Although he missed Monticello, his friends and his family, he enjoyed

"Boots" Thomas, one of the original men to raise the U.S. flag in Iwo Jima, here represented by a historical marker.

college life but could not silence the patriotic desire to join the service that kept tugging at his heartstrings.

The war in Germany and Japan was brewing and escalating. For the people of Boots's generation, the world would forever change when on December 7, 1941, while the German army was freezing in Moscow and while American citizens were sleeping, Japan suddenly pushed the United States into the war by attacking a navy base at Pearl Harbor, Hawaii.

A few months later, Boots would tell his mother in a letter, "All I can think about is Pearl Harbor." Shortly thereafter, he enlisted in the Marine Corps. As in everything he did in his life, he gave it his all. His mother often told him that he was full of vim and vigor.

Boots quickly progressed through the ranks, and at age twenty, he was promoted to platoon sergeant. As his twenty-first birthday approached, he found himself leading a patrol of marines in one of the fiercest and bloodiest battles of the war, on the South Pacific island of Iwo Jima.

On the morning of February 23, 1945, five marines, led by their platoon leader (Boots), raised an American flag over Iwo Jima on top of Mount

Suribachi. It was to be the first American flag ever raised on Japanese soil. Down below, the troops cheered, and the navy's ship whistles went off; it was a moment that all involved would never forget. Marine Sergeant Lou Lowery. with his camera in hand. would take a picture of this memorable moment. Soon after, Boots was interviewed on CBS radio. He was, for the moment, a famous war hero. But the moment passed quickly.

The majority of Americans do not know who Boots was, for that first picture of the marines raising the flag was never published. The Marine Corps, in its infinite wisdom, decided for various reasons that the first photo did not appear professional enough and that the flag was not large enough. It was shelved by the Marine Corps, and a staged second photo was taken just hours later. Knowing that this was a historic and significant event, the small flag that Boots placed on the end of a pipe was removed under the orders of Lieutenant Colonel Chandler Johnson, the battalion commander. The colonel had it in his mind to take possession of the first flag for posterity.

Joe Rosenthal, an Associated Press photojournalist, was climbing up the rough terrain when he looked above and saw four marines seemingly struggling to place a flag on the top of Mount Suribachi. Soon two additional marines arrived to help. This is when he aimed his camera and took his famous photo. This would be the one that went out to newspapers around the world. This photo would be the one reproduced as a bronze statue in the U.S. Capitol and has become the image etched into the world's mind as they recall World War II and Iwo Jima. These six marines would have their names engraved on this statue. These would be the ones who would be remembered as the heroes. The names of Lieutenant Schrier, Sergeant Thomas, Sergeant Hansen, Private Charlo, Private Michels and Corporal Lindberg would be lost forever.

Eight days later, Boots Thomas was killed in action, seven days short of his twenty-first birthday. As he led his squad in battle on March 3, a sniper shot his rifle out of his right hand. Boots did not flinch. The next shot ripped through his mouth, killing him instantly.

Boots and the other marines killed that day were buried on Iwo Jima in a United States Marine Corp Cemetery. Monticello mourned and grieved that this young man had lost his promising future. Even in death, he was not at home. In 1948, three years after his death, Boots did come home. His earthly remains were returned to the United States, and he

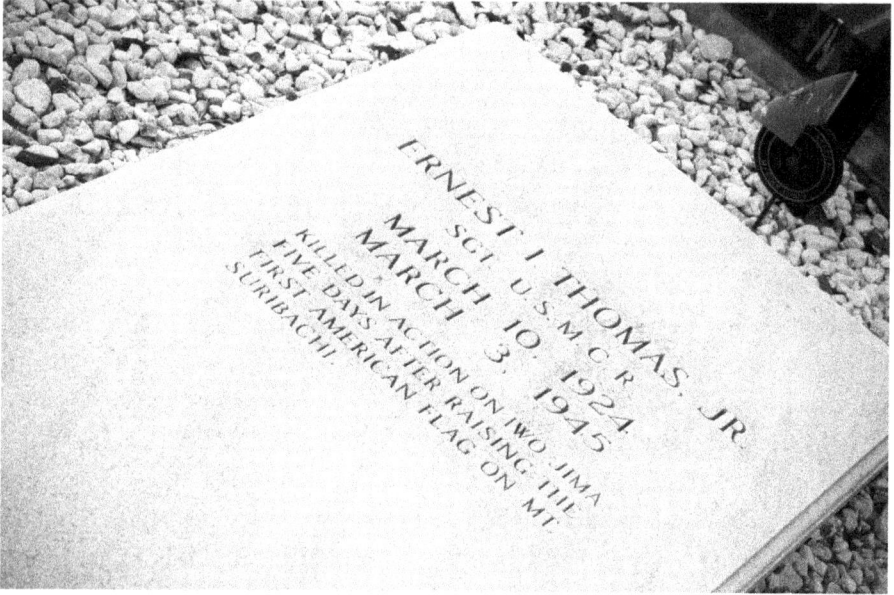

The forgotten hero, Boots Thomas.

was interred at Roseland Cemetery, a forgotten hero. His grave is marked with a marble stone, inscribed with the epitaph: "Killed in action on Iwo Jima, days after raising the first American flag on Mount Suribachi."

In the end, the battle for Iwo Jima would cost nearly seven thousand American lives. For years, many of the marines who fought on Iwo Jima had a saying: "On lonely Iwo buried in black sand are the bones of Marines who fought man to man."

Even Hollywood snubbed Boots and the other first flag raisers when they were not given the credit they so richly deserved. In the 2006 movie Flags of Our Fathers, little-known actor Brian Kimmet portrayed Boots in a scene that was less than a minute long.

If you happen to be taking a stroll through the cemetery, stop by and see his final (or perhaps not-so-final) resting place. He enjoys having visitors. Thank him for paying the ultimate price for your freedoms and tell him that you are sorry that he and his fellow flag raisers did not get the recognition they deserved. If you have music, play some for him (of course, keep the volume low; you would not want to disturb his neighbors). If you are a pretty young lady, stay and chat. You might be pleasantly surprised.

THOSE PESKY CARPETBAGGERS

After the South lost the Civil War, families were thrown into unfortunate circumstances. Many of these families had lost their able-bodied working men in the long war with the North. They had lost the slaves their plantations counted on to turn a profit. Homes, businesses and farms had been plundered or, even worse, burned to the ground. The economy itself was unstable at best. During these tough times, enterprising Northerners began to migrate to the South seeking to make a profit from these unfortunate circumstances. These men would come to town carrying their trademark carpetbags, looking to make a quick profit. These scoundrels came to be known by Southerners as "carpetbaggers." When these men started out for the South, they needed luggage quickly and cheaply, so they chose a carpetbag—usually made by saddle makers who would buy old carpets that still had some life left in them and use the parts that weren't completely worn out to mass-produce these colorful bags in all shapes and sizes. Then they would be sold for just a few dollars in general stores. Carpetbags were the first type of suitcase to be mass-produced.

Carpetbaggers were plentiful during Reconstruction, between 1865 and 1877. Many of these men from the Northern states went to the South because it was so poor after the war that there were many opportunities for a person with even just a little money. Farms could be purchased by paying just the past due taxes for as little as twenty-five dollars. These types of opportunities attracted all kinds of people, from crooks to farmers just looking for honest work. It also attracted con artists and, worst of all, crooked politicians. These unsavory carpetbaggers soon began moving into Monticello, quickly making alliances with freed slaves, getting their hands into politics and disturbing the balance in this very unstable financial, political and social climate. They also began to buy up homes and plantations for pennies on the dollar, forcing many middle-class and even some of the wealthier families from their homes. These men could be cutthroat and malicious at times, trying to get their hands on the properties that piqued their interest. Countless families were driven from homes that had been in their families for generations.

Jefferson County citizens were intolerant of these vile Yankees who, they felt, had come to plunder what was left of their beloved, defeated South. These strangers had brought with them their strange Northern beliefs, and the people of Monticello resented them for trying to push their values on the South. Probably the worst of all these carpetbaggers were politicians who would come in and use their positions in the Reconstruction government to line their pockets through bribes and other disgusting acts—all at the expense of the Southern people.

Calling these unsavory men "carpetbaggers" was meant stir up images of poor transients with their ratty and tattered carpetbags moving in to plunder and steal what they could. However, most of them were actually wealthy to middle class, well-educated men who were simply eager to come set up new businesses and try out the South's economy for themselves. Lawyers, newspaper editors, Union veterans and businessmen were just a few of the entrepreneurs looking to try their luck in the South.

The majority of these carpetbaggers were not nearly as sinister as Southerners saw them. There were many Union soldiers who, after receiving their pay, decided to invest it in this new economic frontier and build a new life in the South. Tales of the wealth that could be made growing cotton brought many to the region. Others were businessmen who leased or purchased plantations and hired freed slaves to work them. Many saw themselves as saviors of the South, people who would bring reconciliation between the North and South by bringing their free labor system to what they considered to be a lazy, undisciplined South. Some carpetbaggers were blacks simply looking to exercise their new rights to pursue freedom and make their own fortune, yet others were Northerners attempting humanitarian efforts to get the newly freed slaves on their feet and return economic stability to the South.

On the street in Monticello referred to by many as "Mysterious Street," people have caught glimpses of a robust man in a dark suit brandishing what appears to be a large carpetbag. He always appears off in the distance, walking between buildings or behind foliage and, at times, down the center of the street. No one has ever been able to approach this gentleman, as he always remains just out of reach and barely visible in the distance. During full moons, when the night is well lit by the silvery light, you can even see the color of his carpetbag: a deep maroon, with large, yellow-gold stripes. He has been nicknamed the "carpetbagger" and is thought to be the spirit of a particularly nasty man who came to take advantage of Monticello's city folk during the late 1800s. After ruining many businesses and running much-beloved and respected families out of their homes, the people had had enough and tried to run the carpetbagger out of town. He refused to leave and seemed hellbent on destroying as many lives as he could before departing. One day, however, it appeared that the pesky carpetbagger had just up and left, taking only his tapestry bag with him. It is strongly suspected that he met with foul play, but no one knows for sure. Perhaps he wanders the streets of Monticello looking for justice—or maybe even in death he is still out scouting for the next victim of his greed.

THE OLD BANK AND HAUNTED ANTIQUES

The Jefferson County State Bank was the first bank to open in Monticello. It was opened in 1889, and by 1901 the bank had a capital of $40,000. D.A. Finlayson was the bank's president and Louis McLain the vice-president. The bank claimed a surplus of $26,000 and reserves of $250,000. For all intents and purposes, the bank was every bit as sound as it claimed. Finlayson remained the president until the bank closed its doors in 1914, due to a panic caused by an apparent misunderstanding when bank cashier R.R. Turnbull left town suddenly and without warning. This caused a run on the bank. Rather than to try to repair the damage caused by the scare, Finlayson decided to liquidate, and the bank was sold.

The old bank is currently a quaint antiques shop called Old Bank Antiques. You can browse and find a wide variety of antiques from many different time periods. Antiques are lovely, and many enjoy browsing for them and buying them. However, be warned. Sometimes, when you buy these old treasures, you may get more than you bargained for. You see, sometimes, if they can't take it with them, ghosts simply stay with their beloved belongings. If ghosts can attach to homes, land or people, it should come as no surprise that they can also bind themselves to an object that was important to them in life.

The old bank is now an antiques shop.

Are you an antiques collector? Many of us love finding great deals on antiques at yard sales, shops and flea markets. Perhaps you have found yourself unexplainably drawn to a certain item or have just felt that you must have it. It may not just be you—it may be an attached ghost that is drawing you to the object.

Be on the lookout for ghostly occurrences after the purchase of new antiques: are you hearing voices or smelling strange odors or aromas? Maybe the plumbing or wiring is on the fritz for no reason at all or you find your mood changing drastically after the new item was brought home. You may have bought yourself a haunted antique.

Here are some tips when shopping for antiques: take the time to examine the object, see how the item feels to you and ask questions (does the seller know the history of the item or any stories about it?). The more you know about the items you bring into your home the better.

Sarah Smith found this out firsthand when she purchased a porcelain doll from an antiques shop: "The moment I saw the doll, I just had to have her. I really couldn't tell you why, I just needed to have that doll." The doll was just a simple dark-haired baby in a white dress. Just a quaint doll that you might imagine a little girl cradling in her arms and pushing around in a carriage. Sarah brought the doll home and placed it on a table by the sofa in her sitting room.

She soon began to notice that every time she passed through the room, the doll had fallen onto the floor. Worried that the doll would get broken, she moved it to the sofa until she could get a stand for it. Still, every time she came into the room, the doll was on the floor again. She even tried laying the doll on its back, but still somehow it would roll onto the floor. Sarah also began to notice that the temperature in the room was so much colder than the rest of the house. This was strange, as the room had always been stuffy in the past. Now it was so cold in there at times that she wondered if her breath was visible. Strange noises could also be heard around the house—the sounds of a little girl giggling and what sounded like skipping in the hallway. After a few months of the ghostly disturbances, Sarah decided to give the doll to a friend who collected dolls. After this, everything returned to normal, and Sarah's home is again quiet and peaceful.

In another instance, a man in Monticello bought an antique ring for his wife. The ring was a present for their second wedding anniversary. It was a beautiful diamond ring from the late 1800s, with an elaborate setting. His wife was crazy about the ring, and as soon as he gave it to her, she wore it everywhere. It wasn't long, however, before her joy tuned to misery, as she found herself suffering from debilitating joint pain. The young twenty-three-year-old woman went to the doctor to see what could possibly be the matter with her. She had always been extremely healthy and had never had problems like this before. Doctors were baffled and could find no explanation for her strange symptoms. They told her that her complaints were like those of a very elderly woman. She began to call in frequently from work and was always tired and in bed. Her husband began to become very concerned for her. They consulted specialists and tried every kind of cure that they could think of, but nothing worked. She lay in bed every night, tossing and turning and praying that she would get well soon.

One day, when the couple was visiting the shop where the ring had been purchased, the clerk struck up a conversation, saying how the ring had belonged to her great-grandmother, who had died at ninety-seven years old. Well, the clerk went on telling them about his dear great-grandmother and how she had worn the ring until the day she died. Suddenly, it dawned on her where all of her pain was coming from. It was coming from the ring, or more specifically from the clerk's great-grandmother, who had decided to stay with her favorite ring. She decided to remove the ring, and her husband locked it up in the safe deposit box at their bank. The next day she felt better, and by nighttime she was back to her old, healthy self; she even got a full night's sleep.

Monticello has some incredible antiques stores, so feel free to come and shop. Just remember to be careful with what you buy.

BIBLIOGRAPHY

Bealer, Alex W. *The Art of Blacksmithing*. N.p.: Castle Books, 2009.

Digital History Project. Monticello Women's Club in 1938, March 3, 2010. http://digitalhistoryproject.pbworks.com/w/page/23751170/ the-digital-history-project and http://digitalhistoryproject.pbworks. com/w/page/23767082/1-early-history.

Florida Historical Quarterly 68, no. 4. "The Read-Alston Duel" (April 1990).

Genealogical information found at the Keystone Genealogical Library, Jefferson County.

Grave markers used at Roseland, the 1827 Monticello Cemetery.

Jefferson County Sheriff's Department, Florida. "Sheriff Thompson Brooks Simkins." Officer Down Memorial Page, Inc. http:// www.odmp.org/officer/16708-sheriff-thompson-brooks- simkins?printview=1.

Jones, Fate. Interview by author, Monticello, Florida, August 2001.

Monticello Drug Company. "Our History." http://www.monticellodrug. com/mdc-our-history.html.

Moore Methodist Museum, Epworth by the Sea, St. Simons Island, Georgia. www.epworthbythesea.org/index.html.

Shofner, Jerrell H. "Antebellum Jefferson County Society." *History of Jefferson County*. Tallahassee, FL: Sentry, 1976.

Smith, Wes. "A Pal Honors the Man Who Planted the First U.S. Flag on Iwo Jima." *Orlando Sentinel,* November 09, 2006.

Tallahassee magazine, July–August 2010.

Turner, Gregg M., and Seth H. Bramson. *The Plant System of Railroads, Steamships and Hotels*. N.p.: Garrigues House Publishers, 2004.

United States Census Bureau records, 1830–1940. www.census.gov.

ABOUT THE AUTHORS

The Big Bend Ghost Trackers team was founded in 2000 and is north Florida's premier professional paranormal group. As paranormal researchers and investigators, they conduct research to find locations that are experiencing paranormal activity and study those locations in a scientific and professional manner. Using the latest electronic tools and other modern detection equipment, along with psychic investigators, they have successfully conducted more than 125 investigations, from a

Team members (from left to right): Melanie Davis, Michelle Cerdan, Christine McVicker and Betty Davis.

About the Authors

haunted castle in Canada to the former Plains, Georgia home of President Jimmy Carter. The Big Bend Ghost Trackers team members have all been witness to and have encountered many paranormal events. Because of these experiences, they treat this subject very seriously and strive to educate, assist and comfort others who are having experiences that they do not understand and need help with. They have been featured on all of the major television networks and in numerous print publications.

Big Bend Ghost Trackers created, owns and operates Historic Monticello Ghost Tours. Throughout the year, a major portion of money made from these tours is donated to local charities. Since 2001, during the month of October, ghost tours are devoted and dedicated to the Monticello–Jefferson County Chamber of Commerce for community improvement, with a donation of 50 percent of all tour proceeds.

Betty Davis works professionally in the field of social services and is a passionate paranormal investigator—the driving force behind Big Bend Ghost Trackers and Historic Monticello Ghost Tours. She enjoys creative writing of nonfiction and historical literature. Having a strong interest in history and historic places, she finds them mysterious and intriguing. She knows that they hold secrets to the past and have defined our future. Experiencing a ghostly encounter while visiting a historic landmark is what first brought her on her journey into paranormal research and investigating the unknown. Betty makes her home in Tallahassee, Florida. She is married and the mother of four adult children; she is also a grandmother.

Christine McVicker is a married mother of two daughters, a professional psychic medium and a paranormal investigator. She has always been interested in the paranormal and has acquired a wealth of knowledge on everything from demonology, spirit communication and magic to hauntings of all kinds. With the ability to communicate with both spirits who have crossed over and those who have remained earthbound, Christine has committed herself to helping both types, struggling with hauntings and spirits who need help crossing over or moving on. An experienced teacher and lecturer in the field of psychic development, her talents and growing reputation are far reaching and much sought after. Christine hails from North Carolina and currently resides in southern Georgia.

www.ingramcontent.com/pod-product-compliance
Lightning Source LLC
Chambersburg PA
CBHW060814100426
42813CB00004B/1064